# Advanced Canine Reproduction and Puppy Care

## The Seminar

Myra Savant Harris

Dogwise™ Publishing

Wenatchee, WA

**Advanced Canine Reproduction and Puppy Care**
**The Seminar**
Myra Savant Harris

Dogwise Publishing
A Division of Direct Book Service, Inc.
403 South Mission Street, Wenatchee, Washington 98801
1-509-663-9115, 1-800-776-2665
www.dogwisepublishing.com / info@dogwisepublishing.com

Graphic design: Lindsay Peternell
Cover photograph: Roberta Anderson
Interior photographs: J. Douglas Harris, LeDonne Santisteven, Gail Herstein, Linda St.James, Cindy Brizes, Marie Westerman, Diane Cifuni

Limits of Liability and Disclaimer of Warranty:
The author and publisher shall not be liable in the event of incidental or consequential damages in connection with, or arising out of, the furnishing, performance, or use of the instructions and suggestions contained in this book.

The information contained in this book is complete and accurate to the best of the author's knowledge. All recommendations are made without guarantee. The author disclaims any liability with the use of this information.

**Disclaimer**
This book was written and published for educational purposes only, and it not intended to take the place of veterinary care. Please consult a veterinarian should the need for one be indicated. The author shall have neither liability nor responsibility to any person, pet, or entity with respect to loss, damage, or injury caused, or alleged to be caused, directly or indirectly by the information contained in this book.

ISBN 978-1-929242-75-7

Library of Congress Cataloging-in-Publication Data
Savant-Harris, Myra, 1944-
  Advanced canine reproduction and puppy care : the seminar / Myra Savant-Harris.
     p. cm.
  ISBN 978-1-929242-75-7
  1. Dogs--Breeding. 2. Dogs--Reproduction. 3. Puppies. I. Title.
  SF427.2.S28 2011
  636.7'082--dc22
                          2010027097

Printed in the U.S.A.

# DEDICATION

It is my pleasure to dedicate this book to the dog breeders throughout the world who health-test their breeding animals with an eye toward eliminating genetically transmitted diseases within their individual breeds. The future of our breeds rests on the shoulders of these men and women. At this time, those of us who breed our dogs thoughtfully and show them enthusiastically do not have a voice. It is my hope that we can become truly unified and mutually supportive as we work together to protect our rights.

# Acknowledgements

I would like to thank the following individuals for their work on this book:

- Cover design: Joann Opel
- Cover photographer: Roberta Anderson
- Chart/Graph Designer: Peter J. Photos
- Photography: J. Douglas Harris, LeDonne Santisteven, Gail Herstein, Linda St.James, Cindy Brizes, Marie Westerman, Diane Cifuni
- Editing: L. Calyn Miller

I greatly appreciate their hard work and generosity. Without the help and technical assistance from my son, Calyn, I could never have written a single book.

# TABLE OF CONTENTS

# My Own Little Laboratory

I am so very lucky. Sometimes I think that I am the luckiest dog breeder on the planet. Not only do I have feedback from the hundreds of dog breeders who have attended my seminars and the thousands of you who have read my books, but also I have the luxury of being part of a very large Yahoo! list that discusses the problems inherent in breeding dogs and rearing puppies. I have the time consuming, but incredibly good fortune to receive emails by the hundreds from dog breeders who are experiencing one problem or another while breeding their dogs. You are my own little laboratory from whom I gather information/data and from whom I receive feedback almost every day. I will be eternally grateful to all of you because your information and your feedback has become my career. Your problems have become my database. I am so appreciative to each of you who have taken the time to write to me with problems and subsequently write again, when my suggestions have translated into puppies for you. I would not trade this experience for anything in the world. Hopefully, having my own little laboratory will translate into gathering good information that I can pass on to all of you, thus making your lives as dog breeders a little more predictable.

# AUTHOR'S NOTE

*Advanced Canine Reproduction and Puppy Care* is my third book published by Dogwise. As the title indicates, it provides the reader with advanced concepts and techniques beyond what were included in my first two books, *Puppy Intensive Care* and *Canine Reproduction and Whelping.* Dog people are always looking for more information and want to improve their skills, so I recently began teaching a new seminar—Advanced Canine Reproduction and Puppy Care. As that has proved successful, it only made sense to write a book containing the information my seminar attendees have been learning. I hope you will find this new information helpful so you can improve your breeding, whelping and puppy care skills. I have provided ample margins for you to take notes as you read.

# A Disclaimer

I do feel the need, given the nature of this book, to add a disclaimer above and beyond what the publishing attorneys always advise. So here goes:

Please remember that the information in my books and seminars is provided to you as one dog breeder to another. I am not licensed to practice as an RN in any state but Washington. I do not dispense information for human health care. I am not a veterinarian. I have learned a great deal about the canine reproduction system from breeding my own dogs. I have learned a great deal from other dog breeders who have taught me. My recommendation to you is that you consult with your vets in all matters concerning the health care of your stud dogs, bitches and puppies. Please consult with your vets in all matters concerning medications, illnesses and problems of all other types.

# INTRODUCTION
# WE DO NOT HAVE A
# VOICE

When I sat down to write my first book, *Puppy Intensive Care,* I did not have a clue that my life would be so consumed from that time forward with trying my best to help other dog breeders accomplish their goals within their breeding programs. As I met more and more dog breeders from all over the US and Canada, I became increasingly impressed with what a hard working group of people we are. "Show Breeders" will travel hundreds of miles a year in order to exhibit the results of their hard work in show rings from coast to coast. If they win a ribbon worth less than a dollar, they are thrilled right down to their toes. If they only win the yellow ribbon in a little puppy class, they go home content and happy that their puppy stood up reasonably well when compared to other puppies his age. It does not take a whole lot to make most of us happy. If there were only four puppies in the class and ours acted like a little jungle animal in the ring winning fourth by default only, for some reason, we are still happy. Once we leave the show grounds, we return home to the life that we have chosen.

The life of a show breeder is understood poorly by people who do not breed and show their dogs, but the life is in most ways identical whether a breeder lives in Toronto or Tacoma. We share so many commonalities. We get up early in the morning to care for our dogs. We feed them, water them, clean up after them, groom them, exercise them and, most of all, we love them. We talk about our dogs endlessly to other doggie friends. No one else will listen. We plan each breeding filled with hopes and dreams of the future. Our intent is not to produce a litter of puppies for sale, but to produce show prospects to keep for showing and, in the future, breeding. We agonize over the decisions made about which puppies to keep and which puppies to sell. We health test and eliminate dogs diagnosed with genetically transmitted diseases from our breeding programs. Good show breeders do not make the headlines. We have nothing in common with puppy millers or even dedicated pet owners. Heaven knows we have nothing in common with the PETA people. The public often confuses us with millers and backyard breeders, but there is no common ground. We are a sub-culture within a culture, totally dedicated to our dogs. We "speak" to our dogs and our dogs "speak back." Are there a few show breeders who neglect and abuse their dogs? Sure. There are a few bad apples in every barrel. We abhor those bad breeders more than anyone does. Fortunately, they are a rarity.

We make choices that millers and pet owners do not make. We choose our own homes based on how dog friendly the property is. Do we have space for a dog room? Do we have enough room for the dogs to run? We choose our automobiles based on how many dog crates we can fit in the back. We choose our clothing, especially the things we wear in the show ring, with an eye toward complementing the colors of our dogs. We look for fabrics that shed dog hair and outfits with lots of pockets to hold the bait we use in the ring. In a time where organizations like PETA and HSUS encourage everyone who wants to share their lives with a dog to adopt an unwanted, unloved dog from a shelter, thousands of dogs breeders have opened their homes and their hearts to foster dogs from their own breeds. These dogs were also unwanted by the pet owners who have turned them back to breed rescue or specialty dog clubs for re-homing. Those organizations and workers provide medical care for these foster dogs, they share their homes and families with them, and they search until the perfect new home is found. They do not euthanize and they do not publicize their rescue programs; they just do what is necessary for the dogs. These wonderful people do not politicize their actions—they just get the job done. It is a privilege to work with those who rescue and re-home dogs. My hope is that I can provide a service to them and to the dogs that we all love so much.

As I have written each book, I have been aware of the many things I do not know or understand about the anatomy and physiology of the canine. However, as I have read articles and books by other individuals, I am reminded of how many misconceptions there are about dogs and how they breed. When I combine my lifetime of owning and breeding dogs with my long career working in labor/delivery and NICU, then add in the hundreds of things that I have learned from other dog breeders, I realize—that in spite of my shortcomings—I have a lot to share with you. It gives me great joy to give something back to the dog community.

Dog breeders, and those wonderful breeders who also do rescue, do not have a voice in this society. Dog breeding is not an activity that has many supporters. Laws are being proposed and passed all the time to prevent us from breeding our dogs. If this were to go unchecked, eventually all puppies will be produced by puppy mills. By puppy millers that do not breed their dogs with health uppermost in their minds. By puppy mills that do not breed dogs with an eye toward a breed standard so that 100 years from now Goldens will look like Goldens, Pugs will look like Pugs, and Cavaliers will look like Cavaliers.

# CHAPTER 1
# THE EVOLUTION OF THE DOG BREEDER

## The Paths We Take

As I have gone about my life as a dog breeder I have met hundreds of other dog breeders, and along the way I have made a sort of discovery. We usually have a lot in common when it comes to our past, present and future as dog breeders. I refer to these similarities as the "evolution of the dog breeder." This evolutionary process has led us along some shared pathways that, without our knowledge, have changed some of the things that we do with our dogs. Those changes have inadvertently led to some reproduction difficulties. Often times, the reproduction problems are self created by turning to science first and then forgetting how natural processes occur. We forget how smoothly things work without us. Sometimes we just forget that dogs are not our hairy children, but an entirely different species. We forget to let them be dogs.

### First we were "Pet people"
Most of us started as pet owners. Either we saw a specific breed that we liked, or we heard about a litter of puppies that was available. We wanted a pet that would be our companion and friend. Frequently, we decided to add a second dog rather quickly, usually because of disputes over "lap time." Each human family member wanted more one-on-one time with the family pet and a second pet seemed to be the solution. When we were pet people, we did the things that pet people do. We occasionally dressed our dogs, and we bought them fancy collars and cute little dog dishes with their names on them. We decorated the dogs and their belongings. Most of us stopped decorating our dogs and their environments as we moved into the show and breeding arena.

### The monster within
At some point, we decided to read a book or two about our specific breed and began to show interest in the local dog shows. Finally came the day when we packed up the dogs and actually ventured out into the dog show world. It was on that fateful day that we awakened within ourselves a sleeping monster—the dog show addict.

The first time we attended a dog show, most of us did not know the meaning of the term "ring time," and a lot of us had a mental image of people leading their dogs around the ring by a leash while a judge decided which dog was the "prettiest." Most of us left that first dog show puzzled by the fact that our beloved Fluffy had been placed as a pet. Clearly Fluffy should have beaten every dog present and brought home all of the ribbons! We had not yet learned about structure or movement, but Heaven knows, at least we were eager to learn. We were not yet aware that Fluffy had a shoulder straight from hell or a tail set that should have astounded us. Instead, we focused on how long Fluffy's ears were or how shiny her coat was.

Over time, we quickly learned all the ins and outs of the dog show world and before long, we really began to get the hang of it. Our competitive streak began to make its way forward, and soon we were spending hundreds of dollars in pursuit of the prize of a piece of ribbon worth pennies. The monster within was slowly raising its sleepy head, sniffing the air and dreaming about portable grooming set-ups and motorhomes. At this point in time, we had not yet become completely ruled by the phrase "do the dogs." But before long our entire lives would be governed by how often we had to return home to "do the dogs," and life as we once knew it was gone. Little did we know, but over time, our dogs and their needs took precedence over just about everything else in our lives.

## Now we are breeders

The number of dogs we kept began to grow. We may have started with a single show dog, but it did not take any time at all before we began looking wistfully at the bitch rings. What was the point of spending all that time just to show one dog? In two shakes of a Poodle's tail, we had a bitch…or two…or three…and, just to be safe, another dog as well. Before long, we began to lust seriously after a puppy to show in the puppy classes or to be more specific, a puppy to show in each of the puppy classes. (And a litter at home, a litter on the way, and a breeding coming up, but I digress.) Of course winning from Bred By was the most fun of all— and how do you win in Bred By unless you are breeding your dogs? We were already well on the evolutionary pathway to the life of the dog breeder.

After a while, our dogs became not only our pets, but also our passion, our obsession, our entertainment and our full time companions. Our dogs meant more to us than any outsider could begin to understand. We began to dress ourselves in various garments featuring our dogs and to decorate our homes with portraits, pillows and ceramic models of our particular breed. When your dogs no longer wear hair bows and eat from dishes with names on them, but your home is covered in dog memorabilia, and you don't own a single piece of clothing or jewelry that doesn't feature pictures of your dogs, you know you've made the leap from pet person to dog breeder. It is all in what and who gets decorated! If you toss in a few bumper stickers and a "Dog on Board" sign, you have won the triple trifecta of dog ownership. Your prize is that ribbon worth a penny.

Somewhere along the way, we probably noticed that old friends no longer phoned us or came to visit, and it became surprisingly obvious that our adult children hated dogs. Who knew? On those rare occasions that we had visitors, we no longer apologized about things like dog hair on the chair or the dog nose in their crotch, and in some weird but comforting way, we began to view dog hair as sort of a condiment/fashion statement: mustard, mayonnaise, catsup, dog hair. Eventually we stopped even noticing it. Never mind about the friends who had deserted us muttering something or other about allergies or the ones who asked pointedly, "Exactly how many dogs do you have?"

Now, we have new friends and love them, except on dog show days when they become the "competition." We try hard on show days to be good about pretending to love them in spite of the times when they win the ribbon worth a penny and we win nothing. These new friends speak our language and we are becoming fluent in Doggie Speak. Words like penis, testicle, tie, egg and sperm, have become an integral part of our vocabulary and, unfortunately, our old friends simply do not have the enthusiasm for us that they used to. Go figure.

## What the heck is a Dog Room?

There dawned a day when we decided to count heads in our kingdom and we found that, almost without realizing it, we had acquired quite a little herd of dogs. Gazing about our furry castle, we saw dogs lounging on the couch, cuddled up on the bed and sitting defiantly in our favorite chair. Sometimes they scooted over a little bit to make room for us and sometimes they did not. We frequently chose to enjoy TV perched on the arm of that chair lest we disturb "one of the kids." (And even now, we scratch our heads in wonderment when they do not view us as the alpha in the pack.) Several of our new doggie friends had "Dog Rooms" and so, finally, we began to explore the option of keeping the dogs segregated just a bit by giving them a "house" of their own so we could reclaim at least part of the house for ourselves. It was time for us to move along to what I call the "Dog Room Concept."

## The Dog Room and musical dogs

The Dog Room gave us back our privacy (no more trips to the bathroom accompanied by twelve inquiring Cavaliers) and most noticeably, some organization to our days. No more herds of dogs running in and out of the doggie doors at will. We began to have a little bit more control over our day and our belongings. Naturally, the dogs needed to be let out first thing in the morning, and often times they needed to be let out in small groups instead of en masse.

Before long, we developed a system. Frequently, one dog or another simply did not get along with one of the other dogs and so, of course, those dogs needed different schedules. Bitches in season needed a different schedule than intact boys. The puppies needed some free time in the yard as well and so rotating the dogs in and out, in and out all day long became a common pastime. We were "Doing the Dogs" from sun up to sun down. Heaven knows, the last thing in the world any dog breeder wants is for the neighbors to be leaning over the fence, counting dogs, so letting them out in groups was a good idea for a variety of reasons. A breeder in Georgia best describes this activity as playing "Musical Dogs," and we were all so used to doing it, we hardly thought about it anymore. However, once we moved to the Dog Room concept and began playing that endless game of Musical Dogs, things began to change for the dogs and those changes have had a surprising effect on the dogs and their ability to reproduce. Our endless game of Musical Dogs has become so natural to us that we no longer even consider the ramifications of how it has affected our breeding programs, although many of us do remember a time when we had larger litters, less troublesome breedings, and more substantial puppies— heavier, more bone and more substance. Let's turn to one of the most important ramifications of our "modern" systems of managing large numbers of dogs.

# Chapter 2
# Let There Be Light

One of the most profound changes that happen when a breeder moves to the Dog Room concept is that all the dogs, especially the bitches, do not get enough pure sunlight during the course of the day. Once upon a time, the girls were free to go outdoors and lounge about in the sunshine as long as they wished; now they are rotated in and out throughout the day to allow all of the dogs in the kennel to have outdoor time, but in a protected and controlled atmosphere.

The fact that sunshine and ovulation is connected is not new information in the animal world. It is well known and documented that mares can be encouraged to ovulate at specific times by the simple addition of eight hours of full spectrum lighting per day. Mares kept in barns full time do not ovulate as regularly as mares kept on pasture. People who own chicken farms that produce eggs instead of meat are well aware of the necessity of keeping the hens under full spectrum lighting. Years ago, when I kept hens, I found that by adding full spectrum bulbs to the hen house, I was able to get egg production from my Leghorn hens to increase dramatically. Without changing their feed or water, production went up from approximately three eggs a week to an easy five eggs per week. People who breed exotic birds all know that birds kept in a bay window with full sunlight for several hours a day will lay far more eggs. It is no secret that full, bright sunlight, or its equivalent from full spectrum light bulbs, will encourage and regulate ovulation—so why isn't it documented or taught to dog breeders? I believe that it is because most vets are not aware of the entire Dog Room concept or the changes that occur when their clients move from breeding one or two bitches to breeding several.

Traditionally, dogs were treated as outdoor animals who were allowed or kept in the house only at the convenience of the family. Dogs were frequently kept in outdoor runs and slept in barns. This was even true for many dog breeders as recently as twenty or thirty years ago. The dogs were fed a very casual diet as well, one that reflected their carnivorous/omnivorous nature. Dogs were loved and shown and bred, but not with the intensity of attention that they now command.

As our society has changed, so have our feelings for our dogs. As those feelings have intensified, the methods and techniques for keeping large numbers of dogs have changed, especially in terms of the amount of time they are kept indoors. Resource materials that are available to breeders do not address the subject of sunlight at all. The science of breeding dogs has not yet begun to reflect the impact of keeping our dogs indoors the bulk of the day. Nor has it begun to reflect the impact that the lack of sunlight has had on showing dogs—particularly black coated bitches—who spend the bulk of their day shielded from sunlight to protect their pigment. The impact of keeping dogs in very warm or very cold climates has yet to be shown. Many dogs are now frequently kept in air-conditioned rooms with windows covered to control the temperature of the room. Dogs that are living in temperate climates are often let out for only brief periods of time to run in shaded or covered runs especially, when their glossy black coats are at risk for being ruined by the exposure of too much sunlight. Is it a significant problem? Yes. It is very significant and very problematic. Hundreds of breeders have reaffirmed this information.

I frequently receive emails that go something like this: "My bitch had her first cycle at one year but she is now 26 months old and hasn't had a season since." Or "My bitch cycles every three to four months, but never conceives." Or "My Doberman, (or Rottweiler or Schipperke) girl has very short seasons, but never stands for breeding and doesn't conceive when we artificially inseminate (AI) her." It is common to hear from dog breeders who had large litters when they first began breeding, but who are now having small litters and many singletons. At first, my response was just the standard reply: that they needed to talk to their vet. After we had exchanged two or three emails, I would discover that the bitch had been seen by more than one vet and had already had several expensive and time-consuming tests.

Eventually, I changed my response and started asking the dog breeder to describe for me in detail how the bitch spent her day, including exercise, activity and diet. After several exchanges I was able to understand what is happening. Many of these bitches were black show girls whose coats were consistently protected from sunshine. Several were little house dogs who refused to go outdoors to potty unless accompanied at all times by their owners, consequently spending very little time outdoors. Many of these "reproductively challenged" girls were bitches living in dog rooms in Arizona, Florida, Alaska and other states well known for their harsh climates. I started troubleshooting by looking for resource materials that related to dogs and sunshine or full spectrum lighting. I found nothing. After reading about horses, hens and canaries, all of whom respond to sunlight by ovulating, I realized that canines are affected profoundly by the amount of sunlight they receive each day.

I believe that sunlight has a twofold effect on bitches and I am quite certain that sunlight or the lack of it affects our boys as well. Mother Nature gets it right most of the time, including her use of sunlight.

For example, when sunlight shines on human skin, it triggers a process which allows skin to manufacture vitamin D. Because the body manufactures it, many who are engaged in research consider vitamin D to be a hormone. It has been difficult to find a direct link between vitamin D and estrogen, but I have come to view the entire process as being similar to the links of a chain. The chain includes sexual maturity, exposure to sunlight on the photoreceptors in the retina of the eye, exposure of sunlight on the canine skin (to a somewhat limited degree), manufacturing of vitamin D, manufacturing of estrogen, the rise in progesterone, the maturity of the follicles containing the egg and finally the ovulation of the egg itself. This egg will eventually turn into a puppy if the bitch is bred and the sperm and egg take a liking to one another.

If any one of the links in that chain is missing, either ovulation will not occur at all or it will occur only sporadically. It may occur, but produce fewer eggs, which will lead to small litters. Therefore, the absence of one of the links in the chain is the first reaction of the canine reproduction system to the absence or shortage of sunlight. The second effect is more of an innately psychological response. When the photoreceptors in the retina of the eye see full spectrum light, whether emitted by the sun or by a specially designed light bulb, called a full spectrum light bulb or daylight bulb, a specific message is sent to the brain. This message is keyed in with the entire reproductive process. When the retina sees the correct kind of light, a pure bright white light containing all of the colors in the spectrum, the brain receives a message, which essentially says, "Breeding now will insure that weather will be warm when you whelp. There will be plenty of food. This is a good time for you to have a nice big litter of puppies." The opposite of that message is received when a bitch is not exposed to adequate sunlight or full spectrum lighting: "If you breed now, the days will be short and dark when you whelp. Food will be in short supply. This is not the best time for you to rear a large litter of puppies; maybe one or two, or maybe none at all." There is no thought process involved. It is a purely evolutionary response to a physiologic occurrence. There is evidence that even human reproduction is related to the length of the days and it is widely accepted that it affects the reproduction of horses, other mammals and all birds.

### How many dog breeders does it take to screw in a light bulb?

Often, the solution to the problem is a simple one. Install full spectrum or daylight bulbs in your Dog Room or areas of the house where the dogs congregate. They also produce a lovely, pure white light that is very easy on the eyes. These bulbs produce more heat than traditional light bulbs, so you will need light fixtures that will allow full spectrum lighting. They are inexpensive and come in either the long tubes similar to fluorescent bulbs or the normal shape of an incandescent bulb. They need replacement about every six months to make sure that the bulb continues to emit the full color spectrum. The best way to find them is to type "full spectrum light bulbs" into your favorite internet search engine and research the different suppliers that come up.

Do not confuse full spectrum with broad spectrum. Full spectrum is the same kind of bulb recommended to prevent the occurrence of "SAD" or Seasonal Affective Disorder, a type of depression that affects humans who live in dark, overcast and rainy geographical areas. Since there is no research material on dogs to guide us as to the amount of time that this light is necessary to encourage appropriate ovulation patterns, I recommend the same amount of time that is recommended for mares: eight to twelve hours per day. The light should be bright enough to cast a shadow and kept on long enough to roughly equate to the length of the days of the seasons. At night, the dog room or runs should be completely dark. In other words, go back to nature. Follow the normal light patterns found in a natural setting and you will find that your bitch will often do the thing that comes most naturally for her to do—ovulate.

Will it work for every single bitch? No, it will not help those bitches who have reproduction problems unrelated to light. Will it work for stud dogs? Yes, it will increase sperm numbers and motility, but it certainly will not "fix" a set of testicles that are no longer functioning because of past injuries or infections. Will it work for a large number of bitches who have experienced irregular cycles or seasons where they do not produce eggs? Yes, it has worked for many bitches and it will work for many more. Breeders have given me information that demonstrates that the bitches who were having irregular seasons will come into season five to eight weeks after the addition of full spectrum lighting. Those bitches are producing larger litters. Will it help to prevent absorption, miscarriage, poor sperm production or any of the other problems that occur with dogs? Yes, it may end up being an inexpensive fix. It is non-invasive and safe for canines of all ages and genders.

The worst thing that can happen when you decide to use full spectrum lighting in your dog room is that you had to spend a little bit of money and an afternoon putting in new light bulbs. At the very least, it falls into the category of can't hurt, might help. Use appropriate light levels in your Dog Room and other areas where the dogs spend the majority of their days as your first line of defense against reproduction problems. Move on to more expensive things and veterinary intervention if five to eight weeks of full spectrum lighting has not brought about improvement.

## What does sunshine or its equivalent do for puppies?

I think that most people realize that vitamin D plays a role in the production of bone mass. Calcium is the main player and is enhanced by the addition of vitamin D. Canines in the wild will keep puppies in the den only until they begin to toddle about. As soon as the pups are walking, mom begins taking them out of the den and encouraging outdoor play. Wild canid pups therefore nap and play outside, even nurse from their moms outside as soon as their little legs can get them up and out of the den. When dog breeders moved indoors to the Dog Room, many of us planned rather nice little puppy nurseries and now keep them indoors because it is a safe and clean environment. We tend to worry a lot more about things like Parvo and Distemper than we do about vitamin D and sunshine.

It seems to me that the same breeders who fret the most about Parvo and Distemper, also fret the most about a lack of bone and substance on their puppies. Another thing that seems to happen more often with puppies left indoors than those puppies who get lots of sunshine, is a tendency to get intestinal parasites. I get emails from breeders who are wrestling with intestinal issues like Coccidia and Guardia in almost every litter. More often than not, a little bit of investigation reveals the fact that breeders who are coping with lack of bone and substance, coupled with skin and/or intestinal issues, are also keeping their puppies indoors most of the time. There is an easy fix for these problems.

You have a number of options. Plan your Dog Rooms to take full advantage of windows if possible. Place your puppy pens in front of windows that catch as much sunlight as possible during the day. Keep full spectrum lighting near your puppy pens if you do not have access to windows. As soon as your babies are toddling, place them in x-pens outside during the day to play on a grassy surface. Unless the weather is very cold or very wet, allow your puppies at least one to two hours a day of healthy fresh air and nice full spectrum light each day.

I think that the best advice that I could ever give you would be to give Mother Nature a try. Try it her way with more fresh air, exercise outdoors and sunshine, just to see if it helps. These little "fixes" are inexpensive and easy to implement. I am not proposing some off the wall behaviors that wouldn't ever happen in nature; I'm proposing that we return back to nature's way when possible. Here is what we know:

- Puppies in nature would spend a lot of time outdoors.
- Vitamin D facilitates bone growth.
- Vitamin D may promote a healthier immune system as well.
- It won't cost you a lot of money.
- Look for healthier skin, more substance and, very possibly, fewer internal parasites.

# Chapter 3
# Dogs are Pack Animals

## Not as Packy as Horses, but Darned Close

We all know that dogs are pack animals, but we are usually quite reluctant to allow them to work out their problems in the way that dogs normally work out their pack issues. Left to their own devices and learning from their moms, a litter of puppies eventually establish a fairly workable system of conflict resolution through the use of growls, posturing, teeth baring, stares and the like, puppies learn how to get what they want, be it a nipple, a warm spot, or a toy. However, this system of keeping order in the puppy pack often breaks down and fights do break out. And once that happens, things can get out of hand and somebody can get hurt. It is not as though they can sit down and have a heart to heart conversation about it followed by a group hug and a couple of verses of Kumbaya. Sometimes dogs will get into a big, noisy, blood-curdling dog fight. Unfortunately, dogs buy into the "kick 'em while they're down" mentality, so there are usually not very many innocent by-standers during a dogfight. Almost everybody gets involved to one extent or another, and even with very small dogs, the frantic owner who is trying to put the dispute to bed will end up with torn clothing, dog bites or worse. However, usually everyone survives if the breeder intervenes quickly enough.

Because of the way that we keep our dogs, they are often simply not able to work out all of the kinks in the pack system and, interestingly enough, those pack issues can lead to reproductive problems. In the wild, the "fittest" dogs in each litter get to breed and pass on their genes. In our Dog Rooms, we choose who gets to breed. The "natural selection" process has been replaced by a "breeders selection" process. If "survival of the fittest," applied to modern dog breeding, chances are that the intact mutt with loads of charm and a hole in his fence would end up being the baby daddy of every puppy in town. (He runs in the sunlight all day anyhow, so for sure his sperm count is simply astounding!)

### Who's the boss?
It helps a bit if we understand the basic structure of the pack and its function. It will help us meet our objectives in dog breeding. Our objectives are quite clear. We want to breed the dog we have chosen to the bitch we have chosen

at the time we determine to be appropriate. We have made those choices for a variety of reasons and we are often paying for the breeding if we make the wrong choices.

Now, how do we go about having successful breedings? We start by identifying which dog is the Big Kahuna in our kennel. Who exactly is the boss? In dog packs, the true Alpha is a bitch. The Alpha bitch's status is not dependent upon her age or her size. It is dependent upon her willingness to fight her way to the top and rule her kingdom fairly but firmly. She may be small and she may be young, but she has been demonstrating her desire to rule the entire kennel ever since you first spied her standing on the shoulders of all of her littermates. Even then, she was exerting her "alpha-ness." She will usually have a Beta bitch in attendance. The Beta bitch is frequently misidentified as the leader of the pack because she is often the one who is seen keeping order in the group.

Here are some things that will help you to identify the two. The Alpha bitch initiates play. She is the dog being chased by the other dogs in a game of run and chase. She is the one who says, "Ok, time to play—so chase me" and she is the one to say, "Game over—I'm tired." She is more often than not the who puppy spends her entire day standing on the shoulders of her littermates. She probably spends some time standing on her mother's shoulders as well. She had designs on the throne even as a toddler. The Alpha bitch does not get her hands dirty. She rarely growls or engages in dogfights. She has minions who handle the dirty work for her, primarily her Beta bitch. The Alpha seeks out the position of highest elevation for her resting place and she often has the best chewies. The Beta bitch is the one who puts down the other puppies, growls at the dogs who need a little bit of reminding about who is who within the social structure of the kennel, and generally keeps order in the group. When you think Alpha bitch, think Queen of England. When you think Beta bitch, think the Queen's thug. If there is an uprising outside the castle, the Queen is not going to grab an uzi and run outside to mow down the rebels. She sends her minions out to do the dirty work while she tends her needlework. This is how your Alpha bitch runs your kennel.

In wolf packs and in groups of horses, we know that dominance is key to deciding who does the breeding. With horses, mares kept in paddocks with very dominant mares will not ovulate as regularly as other mares. I have seen instances of pack behaviors affecting breeding dogs many times and you probably have too if you have been around dogs much. Seeing the behavior is not quite the same as understanding the behavior, so let's start with some basic information to see if we can learn to recognize pack behaviors that might lead to reproductive difficulties.

There are two primary things to remember. First, the dog pack is all about social order and reproduction so both sexes need to be represented. Second, in order for a group of dogs to be a pack of dogs, you have to have certain players and above all, somebody to dominate. So, a group of five bitches does not constitute a pack, neither does a group of spayed or neutered dogs. You need at least two intact girls, two intact boys, and somebody who can fill the role of "underling."

The reason you need at least two of each gender is that within the pack there must be an Alpha bitch who has won her position as alpha and a dominant dog who has fought for and won his position of dominance. If you only have one bitch, for instance, her temperament may not necessarily be one that would have carried her to the position of Alpha bitch within a group. Rather, if there are at least two bitches, it is likely that one would have designs on the role of Alpha bitch. She bides her time until she becomes strong enough to take over the position. Usually there are skirmishes on her way to this position. Sometimes there are outright bloody battles. An Alpha bitch wannabe definitely watches for opportunities to take over that role within the kennel she will often wait until the Alpha bitch is busy nursing and caring for new puppies before she plots her coup. Things really get dicey when two girls of equal strength and intelligence are vying for the same position. If the battles rage on without a clear winner, you will actually be happier if you can place one girl, perhaps with some of the breeding rights to her, rather than let the girls jockey endlessly for position. Once things have been resolved, watching carefully you will see signs that there is a new queen in town. The new alpha will come in from outside last, eat first from a communal bowl and even demonstrate a new attitude of total confidence. She carries herself differently. Once an Alpha bitch is firmly entrenched in her role, you will not continue to see skirmishes or witness a lot of quarrelling. A good Alpha bitch, worthy of the position, rules with a gentle paw. She has a Beta bitch to do the heavy lifting for her.

## You want me to stand for…HIM? Get outta here!

Along the way, the Alpha bitch has become well acquainted with the dogs within the kennel. She knows who is the most submissive, who is at the bottom of the social rung in the doggie ladder, and she knows who is dominant. If you make a decision to breed your Alpha bitch to one of your young boys that has shown promise in the show ring, but is clearly not one of the dominant boys, you may well run into difficulties with the breeding. In effect, you have asked the queen of England to stand and flag for the pool boy. Queens often have other plans and besides, she is the alpha and in her mind, she gets to choose the sire for her litter. It is at these times that dog breeders may need to revert to the skill of collecting sperm and performing an AI followed by an artificially simulated tie.

The stud dogs within a kennel also have a hierarchy. There will always be a dominant boy and at least one dog who is submissive to that dominant dog. The boys do not appear to have a second in command. When a dominant boy breeds a girl within the pack, he elevates her position within the pack. If he has decided that she simply is not a bitch that he chooses to elevate, he may decline to breed her. If she is a new bitch who has been sent to you for breeding, he may hesitate because he doesn't understand her pack position or standing. If the bitch is extremely shy and timid, he may decide that he simply does not want to elevate her position within any pack. When an experienced stud dog declines to breed a bitch, it is often a pack issue for him. Again, a watchful dog breeder can quickly revert to the skills necessary to collect a dog and inseminate a bitch followed by an artificially simulated tie. I'll be discussing the tie in Chapter 4, so just keep reading, don't stop now.

# CHAPTER 4
# THE LITTLE STUD MUFFINS

## Our Boys, the Dogs of the Species

There has never been an example of such blatant overkill as the discrepancy between the numbers of eggs produced by the bitch versus the numbers of sperm produced by the dog. Mother Nature tends to be rather thrifty, rarely wasting her resources, so I suspect that the fact that sperm numbers are overwhelming when compared to egg numbers is because the system requires it in order to guarantee perpetuation of the species. From human studies, we know that sperm (a reminder: *sperm* are the swimmers; semen is the total ejaculate containing sperm plus prostate fluid) are in a constant state of development. The best way to visualize this is to imagine a fish farm with many tanks. Some tanks contain the tiny little "fry," some tanks contain the medium and slightly larger fish and the larger tanks contain the largest fish, fully mature and often used for the reproduction end of things. There are fish at many stages of development at the fish farm, but only the fully mature fish can reproduce. That's how the sperm in your stud dog's testicles are organized. There are sperm at many different stages of development at locations within the testicle and there is a large "reservoir" of fully mature sperm ready for ejaculation, the majority of which can penetrate an egg.

An adult dog at his sexual prime with no reproduction issues probably has somewhere around 80% good quality sperm in a collection unless he has had a lengthy period of "sexual rest." If those sperm have been swimming around in the reservoir playing Marco Polo for a few months then undoubtedly some of them have died of old age. Sperm that just sits around in the reservoir begin to develop anomalies, usually in the heads (two heads, bent heads, shriveled heads, heads gone), but sometimes in the tails too (mainly just gone, but also bent, curved or damaged). It makes perfectly good sense that it may take a few sperm collections in order to get the stud dog's reservoir of sperm back to good quality—so out with the old, in with the new.

Stallions that have had a period of "sexual rest" may require as many as ten semen collections before the dead or deformed sperm are gone and the collection returns to full quality. Humans also have relatively poor quality sperm if ejaculation does not take place regularly. (So, as it happens, masturbation—

once thought to make men insane, blind and acne prone—also keeps them at their reproductive best. All primed up but with so few women to take on a crazy blind man with pimples. Go figure.) A stud dog would require at least three collections spaced over five to seven days prior to the day of the actual collection used for the breeding, chilling or freezing in order to make sure that the quality of the collection is at its best. In the world of the stud dog and other mammals, the old saying "use it or lose it" has a valid application when it comes to sperm. Clean out the reservoir from time to time or it will contain millions of unusable, deformed, elderly and dead sperm. They will be unable to penetrate the eggs.

The large "reservoir" certainly has enough sperm for six to ten collections, but once it's on empty it will take at least three weeks, possibly longer, for the production within the little "nursery" tanks to begin to fill again. You can see now that the dog breeder must walk a fine line between under using the stud dog's resources and over using them. Lengthy periods of "sexual rest" are almost certain to lead to decreased fertility as would using the dog daily for a lengthy period of time. Certainly, you could use your stud dog for breeding six to ten days in a row, but there is rarely a valid reason for doing so and you would run the risk of having smaller litters after a while. If there are multiple girls requiring the services of the stud dog, the breeder is far better off checking progesterone levels on each bitch and having the stud dog service each girl only one or two times at the appropriate state of egg development. (I will get to that in another chapter. Stay tuned.)

The sheer numbers of sperm are staggering. It is difficult to imagine what those numbers mean and how it all fits together in a way so that dog breeders can utilize the information in their day-to-day breeding decisions. If we can put those numbers—millions, hundreds of millions, billions (even the word trillion has come into common usage in the last few years)—into some frame of reference that is more understandable, it becomes easier to comprehend how sperm versus egg is one of the most striking examples of overkill in nature. Will it surprise you as much as it surprised me? Will it really take your breath away and knock your socks off? Let's go see!

## I'm staggered, breathless, sockless and I need a really comfy chair

Let's say that you have decided to count to one million at the rate of one number per second before you get out of your chair. You would be sitting in your chair for 278 hours—almost twelve days. Now, let's set our sights a bit higher and decide to count to a billion at the rate of one number per second. That would take you almost 32 years. Now, take a deep breath and start counting to a trillion at the rate of one number per second. You'll need that deep breath because it will take you almost 32,000 years to count to one trillion at the rate of one number per second. (I can just see some of you scurrying off to get your calculators. "She's wrong! That can't possibly be right! Thirty two thousand years?") When you put numbers into a time frame that you can understand you begin to get a real understanding of the wonders of canine sperm.

A small toy dog will ejaculate somewhere in the neighborhood of 200 million to 300 million sperm per ejaculate. A larger toy dog can ejaculate around 400 million sperm per ejaculation. (The population of the United States is, at present, under 400 million.) Mastiffs can ejaculate around a billion sperm per ejaculate, give or take. (The population of the planet is, at present, well a little under 7 billion.) Meanwhile, the bitch is something of a lazy little piker as she ovulates anywhere from only one egg to twenty or so, depending on her age, condition, breed and several other factors.

Why is there such a difference in those reproductive numbers? I'm sure it has to do with many factors, the first of which is that if dogs were unfenced, unfettered and left to roam about breeding at will, then the concept of "survival of the fittest" would step in and there would be certain stud dogs who would do the bulk of the breeding. These dominant males might be called upon to service several bitches a week and nature has designed them to be able to do that should the need arise. Were dogs to be able to take matters into their own little paws, there would be a spirit of competition and many confrontations over the right to breed. The winner would probably not be a Yorkie or a Chihuahua since he would need to take on all challengers for reproductive rights. He would need some size behind him. Chances are the winner would be a medium to large sized dog with a strong inclination to reproduce. This dog would not shy away from a fight, but neither would he waste energy looking for a fight. This dog would need many sperm in order to be fit to breed multiple bitches.

So, aside from perhaps meeting the needs of multiple bitches, what are some of the other reasons why dogs produce such mind boggling numbers of sperm? Some of the reasons simply have to be anatomical. The bitch has a rather long vaginal canal when compared to a human. The human vagina is roughly three inches long with some flexibility and stretch built into it. How do I know this? Because of the thousands of vaginal exams I've done on moms who were preparing to deliver. Vaginal exams done with index and middle fingers are always quite successful and reach the targeted cervix. Bitches have a longer distance from the vulva to the cervix than a human does—including even some of the toys. (Look at the length of our AI rods.) Bitches have two uterine horns that reach upward into their bodies instead of one small, pear shaped uterus that barely rises above the level of the human pubic bone. Their fallopian tubes sit near the top of those horns at quite a distance from the cervix. They usually produce more eggs than would be normal for a human. When we combine all of those factors—longer vaginas, two uterine horns instead of one (some of which are quite lengthy) and more eggs needing to be fertilized, it becomes obvious why there is such an abundance of sperm in the canine. His sperm need to swim a longer distance to make it to the fallopian tubes attached to two horns and they need to be numerous enough to fertilize many litters within a short period of time.

A young dog will begin the production of sperm anywhere from approximately seven months of age for a toy size dog to approximately fourteen months for the largest dogs. The sperm isn't very good quality at first and may even be quite bizarre looking as the manufacturing plants (those two testicles) begin their work. The boy will begin the manufacture of sperm about the time he reaches roughly 85% of his adult size. He may have started a meaningful relationship with his stuffed toys or pillows a few months prior to the time he actually has a few sperm, but this is usually just a developmental stage and will end when the dog has been used for breeding the first time. It is more a problem with pet boys who have been neutered than for stud dogs. Stud dogs know the difference between your leg and a bitch in season. Pets dogs don't always seem to. Pets with bad manners retain a fondness for our legs throughout their lives. The intact dog reaches his prime age for reproduction at somewhere between eighteen months or so for toy dogs to 24 to 30 months of age for the largest sized dogs. He will remain at the ready for breeding for most, but not all, of his life. While he may be still quite willing as he ages, the success rate with older boys tends to decrease. There is no evidence that his age leads to birth defects in his puppies however, so if an older boy is able he can be used as a stud dog if you wish.

## Aging: Life span and penetration

Age affects the fertility of stud dogs just as it affects the fertility of bitches. I hear from hundreds of dog breeders a year who relate their experiences. The problems I hear about often go something like this: "The vet did a semen collection and I saw the sperm on the microscope slide. He felt that there are plenty of sperm, but my older boy has missed on several bitches. What do you think the problem could be?"

What I know and can share with you is this—you can see sperm on a microscope slide but you can't see *life span* and you can't see *acrosomes*. Life span and acrosomes are at least two of the things that go missing as a dog ages. I suspect that older dogs who still have sperm that appear to be healthy when viewed using a regular microscope, but have fertility issues in spite of this are, indeed, suffering from the effects of aging. Their sperm probably does not have the life span of sperm from a younger dog in his prime. Studies have shown that fresh sperm have been retrieved from the reproduction tract of a bitch as long as ten days after being placed there. (What the studies did not show was whether the sperm was capable of penetrating the egg. I suspect not.) For the purposes of a dog breeder, fresh sperm (as opposed to chilled or frozen) should be considered to have a life span of five full days once placed within a bitch assuming the dog is in his prime or, in the case of an older boy, has sired litters within the last six months.

Sperm undoubtedly has a longer life span than five days, and if that sperm was deposited by the next door neighbor's mutt, it will most certainly live almost indefinitely, but you should base your breedings with five days in mind. If you are going to use an older boy, you should time those breedings for the days when the eggs are fully ripened, but not yet dying and dead; from late on day three to the end of day four following ovulation. The sperm from an older boy may only have a life span of a day or two. You should consider asking your vet to do a surgical insemination of the older dog's freshly collected sperm to maximize your chances that his sperm will live long enough to get to the eggs and penetrate them. Now, assuming that the sperm has lived long enough to reach the eggs; will those sperm still have the all-important acrosomes necessary to penetrate the eggs? The acrosomes are the little cap-like structures that cover the head of the sperm. They contain important enzymes, which facilitate the penetration of the egg. Acrosomes are visible under electron microscopes, but not a regular microscope in a vet's office. Your decisions will need to be based on knowledge and information about the stud dog; combined with what the vet can see using a microscope. Before you pay a stud fee or plan an important breeding that involves an older stud dog, you need to have valid information about the litters he has recently sired. If he is still siring litters into old age, his age becomes a true asset to the breeder because it is a testament to his longevity, health and vigorous immune system. These older boys are very valuable to their breeds and are under-utilized.

## If you are going to freeze—freeze 'em young
When dog breeders first began freezing sperm in the 1980s, the general consensus was that breeders should use the boy naturally while he is young and once he begins to get older they should consider freezing his sperm. A lot of frozen inseminations fail because the sperm used come from older boys. The lesson to be learned is that to maximize your success you'll want to begin collection and freezing while the boy is in his prime. It should go without saying that if a boy was collected when he was two and three years of age, but was then diagnosed with a serious genetically transmitted disease when he was four or five, the sperm which was collected and frozen needs to be discarded from your breeding program.

I meet people at my seminars who disagree with my information about aging and how it affects reproduction in both dogs and bitches. I have been told of a case using frozen sperm taken from a twenty year old stud dog and inseminated into an eighteen year old bitch resulted in a litter of seventeen puppies, all of whom are multi-champions. The elderly bitch is now 21 and is in whelp with her fifteenth litter. I know that surprising and unexpected things happen in the world of dog breeding, but I like to teach the general rules of how things work and not focus too much on the occasional, exceptionally pleasant surprises. Old stud dogs usually begin to lose fertility before they begin to lose sperm.

## The life span of chilled and frozen sperm
This is a topic fraught with disagreement. If you do a bit of research, you will find many sources that disagree with my particular take on the life span of chilled and frozen sperm *once placed in the bitch*. However, there is very little disagreement about how long the sperm lives in the freezer or in the test tube. Once the sperm has been collected and prepped for freezing, it will probably live longer than you will as long as it is never thawed and refrozen. (Put a tiny container of liquid nitrogen and sperm in my coffin and I can keep right on breeding dogs in Heaven if I can find a vet who intends to keep on

doing surgical inseminations all day instead of sitting on a cloud playing a harp.) Kept at the correct temperature (and your household freezer is not cold enough) it will live indefinitely.

Once sperm has been collected and prepped for chilling and shipping, things are a little bit more uncertain. With a good extender, some reproduction vets say that the chilled sperm will live in the tube for seven full days providing it remains at the appropriate temperature. To be on the safe side, I do not think you should count on more than three days life span in the shipping container, but it certainly appears that it can live for seven under the right circumstances. The big area of contention concerns the life span of chilled sperm or frozen sperm once within the bitch. I think that everybody agrees that freezing and chilling cuts into the life span significantly; we just disagree about how deeply it cuts. My guidelines are the most conservative.

Why do you suppose my guidelines might be tighter than that of you vet? Perhaps chilled and frozen sperm does live as long as many of the reproduction experts claim—and longer than I believe—but this is my response to the issue. They do not own our bitches. It is not their breeding that missed. It is not their hopes and dreams of those championship puppies that are dashed to the floor when a breeding does not result in puppies. It is not their money that pays for the stud fee, the transportation of the semen, or the vet expenses on both the collection and the insemination end of the breeding. It is ours and if a breeding fails because of crummy timing, nobody gives us our money back and nobody can make those hopes and dreams return; at least not for six months to a year. It behooves us to speak up, set our own timing guidelines, and insist on the timing that you want to follow when planning *your* breedings.

When you get to the chapter on the bitch and particularly the life span of her eggs, you will see how these pieces of information can combine to give you the maximum shot at having puppies. Plan your breedings based on your knowledge about the life span of the sperm (fresh, frozen or chilled) and the life span of the egg. You may not be willing to pay for an insemination on Friday that should have been done on Saturday or Sunday, if you are willing to go with the shorter life spans that I believe to be correct. Here are the life spans that I know to be effective and that I know to end up with the highest success rates when using chilled and frozen sperm.

### Chilled sperm will live inside the bitch for approximately twelve hours

You will find sources that state that chilled sperm lives in the bitch as long as three full days. Somebody is wrong here. There is a big difference between twelve and 36 hours. Most of the same sources that state that chilled sperm lives for three days also teach that fresh sperm lives five days. If it takes two days for the shipment and lives for three days in the bitch these experts are giving chilled sperm the same life span as fresh. Nothing could be further from the truth and all you have to do to realize it on your own is to visualize cold sperm on a microscope slide. They do not move like fresh sperm. Something happens in the chilling process that cuts into their life spans. Plan your breedings centered around a life span of twelve hours on chilled sperm. If you can afford it, consider a surgical implantation using that precious chilled sperm and you will really begin to maximize the potential for a successful breeding. It is possible to use a vaginal insemination and it is possible to use a trans-cervical insemination, but for maximum success using chilled sperm, try a single surgical insemination and time it keeping in mind that twelve hour life span.

## Frozen sperm will live inside the bitch for about one to two hours—tops

I have seen claims that frozen sperm lives for 48 hours inside the bitch, but the most frequently found sources say that it lives for 24 hours once placed inside the bitch. It actually lives about one to hours once inside the bitch. For that reason, you will need to plan to do a single surgical insemination. (Run like the wind from a vet who wants to do *two* surgical inseminations a day or two apart. Believe me, they are out there. Sprint away from this person as fast as you can because there is a clearly a real misunderstanding about wounds and how they heal. You cannot separate a wound that has begun the process of closure and expect it to heal normally after it is closed a second time.)

When sperm is only going to live one to two hours once it is placed, your goal is to get the sperm as close as possible to the location that contains the eggs (the fallopian tubes) and to make sure that those eggs are ripe and fully ready for penetration. A single surgical insemination at the right time is the ticket to puppy breath. My favorite reproduction vet in the world, Dr. Cindy Smith, says that success when using chilled and frozen is about three things— Timing, Timing and Timing—and her success rate when using chilled and frozen is enviable. Plan your breedings using frozen sperm based on a life span of one to two hours and coordinate that life span with the life span of the egg and you will maximize your chance of success. The decreased life span of chilled and frozen sperm does not reflect on its quality or its genetic health; it is strictly a function of what chilling and freezing does to sperm. When we use chilled and frozen semen, we are tampering with Mother Nature—and any time we tamper with Mother Nature there is a price to be paid. In the case of chilled and frozen sperm, the price to be paid is decreased life span.

## How we collect is important, too

When you collect sperm from a dog, he can either mount, using a bitch as a teaser, or he can be standing on all four legs. If he is standing on all four legs, the procedure is called a "ground collection," and if he is in the mounted position, you would refer to that as a "mounted collection." Studies on stallions have indicated that the number of sperm is higher when the stallion is collected using a mounted position. There it is—that pesky tampering with Mother Nature thing again since stallions in nature would mount the mare. (Mother Nature seems to have figured this stuff out a long time ago.)

Avoid the use of germicidal soaps or Betadyne on the penis prior to breedings. When collecting stallions, the use of germicidal soaps or Betadyne can lead to fungal skin infections on the penis. Normal defense bacteria are destroyed, leaving other bacteria to proliferate and cause lesions. A simple warm rinse using homemade saline solution is sufficient to remove the light coating of smegma that is sometimes on the penis of the dog (and for you horse people, it is not nearly as unpleasant as cleaning the stallion of his smegma). Saline solution is made by mixing sixteen ounces of distilled water with one teaspoon of plain, non-iodized salt and one half teaspoon of baking soda. Mix it fresh prior to using and make sure it is about 95 degrees or so.

## A word about heat

Obviously a dog and his testicles can survive bitter cold, as witnessed by those wonderful dogs that run the Iditarod every year. Heat, however, is another matter. A dog will usually survive his encounter with heat, but his sperm may not. Most mammals have a muscle (called the "cremaster" muscle for those of you who like details) that allows the testicles to lower away from the body when they get too warm. The same muscle raises the testicles up inside the body if the dog is in standing water over 110 degrees or so because the body temperature is cooler than the temperature of the water surrounding the testicles. Testicles tend to be roughly three degrees cooler than normal body temperature for most mammals. For humans with an average body temperature of 98.6, the testicles do their best job of producing sperm when they are at 95 degrees. For dogs, it is most likely around 98 degrees. (The lesson learned here is that no matter how appealing you may find Speedos to be, it is always a good decision to keep them away from Fido, Spot or Windsor. I cannot emphasize this enough both in the testicular sense and in the interest of good taste in fashion.) I cannot help but speculate that this lower body temperature thing is also why newborn puppies (the males of which have testicles inside their bodies) need to be kept at a temperature of 95 and the dog only begins to have body temperature of 99-100 degrees after his testicles have fully descended. Nature protects testicles from heat in all circumstances.

Let us take a moment to review these first four chapters and to list the major things you can do to protect the fertility of your valuable stud dogs. Here is what I propose to you:

- Make sure your dogs get plenty of fresh air, exercise and *sunlight.* In the absence of sunlight, install full spectrum lighting.

- See to it that none of the other boys (or girls for that matter) are making your dog's miserable within the pack. If pack interaction becomes violent or too ugly, your stud dog's reproduction freedoms may well be affected and not in a positive way. Consider placing a dog that is constantly on the wrong end of pack interactions.

- Do not scold your boy for maintaining his meaningful relationship with his stuffies or for trying to hit it off with the bitches. Praise him, but gently lead him away from dinner guests and small children. Practice is one thing—public practice is another.

- If you are planning to use your boy, do not wait until he is a fully mature dog. Once his health testing requirements are completed and he is old enough to meet the regulations of your various dog clubs, use your boy. If dogs do not breed at an early age, they frequently will not breed at all. Use it or lose it should be our motto. Assess his litter carefully and with an unbiased eye. You may decide that this is a great dog to show, but not necessarily a great dog to breed. It happens and it should happen more often. Both show dogs and stud dogs bring positive things to the kennel.

- Train him to ejaculate for collection in the mounted position when possible.

- If he has not been used recently, collect and destroy at least three collections.

- Protect the semen from drying out, from heat, and from cleaning supplies of any kind. If using fresh semen, inseminate the bitch as soon as possible. If you are checking its viability on a microscope slide, warm the slide to your own body temperature prior to putting semen on it. Cold glass slides have led to more diagnosis of poor quality sperm than any other single factor. Warm the slide and you will not have that problem.

- If you plan to freeze his semen, collect him while he is young and ask a vet to assess the vitality of his sperm after being frozen for one year. There is no reason to keep paying the fees if his sperm is no longer able to penetrate the eggs.

- Supplement the diet of your boys with Glycoflex and Acetyl L Carnitine to increase sperm numbers and motility.

- Insure that whether you do a natural breeding or an AI, you allow adequate time for a tie or a simulated tie to facilitate breeding successes. Take your time.

- Protect the stud dog's testicles from excessive heat whether from lying on overheated surfaces, standing in warm water or using a blow dryer on their rear ends while grooming.

- Avoid any drying coats or grooming aids that hold the testicles close to the body.

- Practice good dental care on a regularly scheduled basis. Infections of the mouth often go undetected and can lead to infertility and probably cardiac disease.

- Try to protect a potentially important boy from kennel messages that repeatedly tell him he is not a dog to be used for breeding. Build his confidence.

# CHAPTER 5
# THE TIE IS IMPORTANT

## It's Important. It's Important. It's Important!

Mother Nature does not make mistakes. Sometimes she seems to take the long away around a problem, but she does not make glaring errors. At first glance, the tie between breeding males and females in the canine family certainly appears to be a gross error in good judgment. There they are, in plain view of everyone—including predators; locked in a most unbecoming stance, rear end to read end. When locked in the tie, they are fair game to anyone passing by and indeed, male wolves have been observed attacking other male wolves locked in ties, unable to protect themselves or escape.

Canids appear to prefer breeding at night under the cover of darkness and with darned good reason. The darkness affords them a small measure of protection while they remain in a tie, vulnerable to all threats. I suspect that the tie is an anatomical requirement necessitated by the length of the body and uterine horns of the bitch and the number of eggs that she has ovulated. Sperm needs to have adequate time to make its way up that rather long vagina, and upward through those two lengthy uterine horns. Furthermore, enough of them have to make it to the target to insure that all of the eggs are fertilized. The tie is the key to success for the canine and we breeders have, all too often, been guilty of relegating its importance to the back burner.

During my childhood, when I was around many dogs, I viewed the "tie" as being sort of a game that dogs played. I did not know what the tie was all about and as I remember it, I thought that they were playing "circus." Once I got old enough to understand that it had to do with breeding, I was a little bit uncomfortable being around dogs in a tie. Those days are long gone.

During the first several years that I bred dogs, I looked upon the tie as something of a waste of time. (Come on people—the clock is ticking and I have stuff to do! Tick Tock.) I was willing to concede that there was probably a bigger purpose to this copulatory lock, but I did not really know what it was. Once I learned how to collect sperm and inseminate a bitch, I was just glad to be able to cut to the chase and save a little bit of time.

My problem at that point was that I would occasionally miss my breedings when I did AIs— even when I had progesterone levels as my guide for timing, and I knew that the placement was good and the stud dog was fertile. It seemed to me that whether sperm was deposited at the cervix by the penis or by an AI rod, the result should be the same. The results, however, were not always the same and if I missed a breeding, it was always the AI that was the culprit, never the natural breeding with the tie.

A few years back I asked a vet why it was that I would miss on AIs with sperm deposited at the cervix just as the penis would have delivered it. She replied that she was not sure, but that that vets missed on AIs more often than natural breedings too. This is exactly the kind of thing that drove me to learn more. It just did not make sense that if the AI rod could deposit sperm at the cervix just as the penis delivered sperm to the cervix, the AI would lead to failed attempts at breeding when natural breedings did not. Placement is placement, isn't it? Turns out, not so much. Since then, I have spent a considerable amount of time trying to understand what it is about the tie that facilitates successful breedings. What is the contribution of the tie to the species?

Dogs belong to the family of *Canidae* along with wolves, coyotes, foxes, jackals and dingoes. Some scientists classify them as belonging to the species *Canis Familiaris* while others refer to dogs as a sub-species of *Canis Lupis;* the wolf. (All I can say about that is that anybody who believes that dogs are only a sub species of wolves has been spending way too much time with Huskies and not nearly enough time with Cavaliers.) The males in the canid family are involved to one extent or another in the rearing of the young, but dogs fall into the group that is involved the least of all. Wolves, by contrast, appear to take the most active male parenting role, bringing food home to the nursing female and regurgitating food and water to the young. Stud dogs play only a limited male parenting role, often exhibiting little interest in the puppies until they are old enough to play, and even then not demonstrating more interest in their own puppies as opposed to other puppies within the kennel. Then again, they are just as likely to growl at puppies in the group as to play with them, so even their contribution in that field varies. Perhaps this has to do with the way dogs are kept in houses or kennels as opposed to running wild, but it can hardly be denied that it would be a rare stud dog indeed who opted to feed a female caring for young rather than feeding himself. Dogs are not monogamous as are most of the other canids so there is little incentive to feed either the bitch or her puppies.

The tie itself is an important contribution to the perpetuation of the species and especially to the genetic contribution that each individual stud dog makes. The tie is the stud dog's primary contribution. It is geared toward making sure he is the sire.

### So, how come he gets to tie and I get to lick bottoms?
There is no doubt that on the parental end of things, the bitch's job is more labor intensive and time consuming than the dog's, but his reproductive behaviors and anatomy does indeed make an important contribution to the

species. His anatomy is a bit different from almost all mammals because of the "bulb" that lies at the uppermost portion of the penis, right next to the abdomen. Much of the research done on wild canids suggests that the tie is created by a swelling at the tip of the penis. I cannot state this with absolute certainty that this is true for jackals—having had no experience collecting their sperm—but I am pretty sure those researchers did most of their observations with binoculars versus "hands-on" work. I believe that all canine bulbs are at the proximal (closest to the abdomen) end of the penis. After the dog has entered the bitch, the bulb begins to swell. It can easily be the size of a plum on a toy dog and as large as an apple on a larger one. While the bulb is swollen to its full size, the dog is unable to retract it because it is held firmly in place by the vaginal ring of the bitch. This is the tie.

Probably many bitches out there regularly grumble to each other: "Dog, He work from tie to tie but Bitch will work until she dies." Or maybe some other variation of the old saying that "Man, he work from sun to sun but woman's work is never done." The stud dog's contribution when compared to the weeks of gestation, the hours of labor, and the weeks of nursing, bottom licking and weaning put in by the bitch probably seems insignificant at a glance, but it is very important. The tie has two primary functions.

We have all seen what happens when groups of dogs run loose. There is often a bitch in heat at the head of the pack followed by a little herd of males in hot pursuit of her sexual favors. Dogs are not monogamous, although dogs and bitches frequently "pair off" within a kennel and become deeply attached to one another. This does not meant that they will not breed with other dogs. They will breed indiscriminately as anyone who has ever seen a dachshund/shepherd mix can attest. Keep in mind that dogs do not mate with sexual pleasure in mind. We do not actually know how much enjoyment they actually find in the act of breeding. The one thing we understand is that they are highly motivated to complete the act. They are engaged in a fight to perpetuate themselves.

When a stud dog breeds, he places his penis within the bitch before it is erect. The penis is not erect nor is the bulb engorged. Dogs have a small bone in their penis that enables them to have intromission (enter the bitch) prior to erection. If the dog waited until he was fully erect before intromission, his bulb would not make it past the vaginal ring that is a short distance inside the vagina. When this occurs, it is called an outside tie. The bulb of the penis is outside of the bitch's body and the dog must be held into place for the breeding. Sometimes outside ties are successful, but more times than not, they are unsuccessful.

Normally, the dog enters the bitch while still small but firm. Once he has mounted the bitch and begun the brief thrusting time, he quickly becomes erect. The penis increases its length so that the tip comes closer to the cervix and the bulb engorges and becomes trapped by the involuntary action of the vaginal ring. These are the anatomical characteristics of the tie. Studies have shown that by the time the stud dog has lifted his back leg and is no longer mounting the bitch, the sperm has been deposited and all that is left is the pulsating action of the prostate fluid which is useful in propelling it through the cervix. Some books I have read refer to the semen as "pumping" and "churning" inside the bitch. I suspect men wrote these books. Having watched ejaculations, I have noticed that the sperm actually just drips into the collection device with no pulsated force behind it at all, and the prostate fluid, which does have a pulsating force just sort of spurts out in weak streams. What a man would call "pumping and churning," a woman would call "dripping and squirting." I'm just sayin!

By the time the tie is over, the bulk of the sperm have crossed over the cervical barrier and are within the uterus at the level of the fallopian tubes. The dog has done his best to insure that his sperm has fertilized the eggs within the bitch. If sperm reach the egg before they have ripened, they just kick back there in the fallopian tubes and wait for the time when penetration of the eggs can occur. It is for this reason that it is possible to have puppies from more than one stud dog in the same litter. Each stud dog, however, has done the best he can to insure that sperm carrying his own DNA has reached the eggs before another breeding can take place. He was also instrumental in bringing sperm to egg by yet another useful tool. His semen contains prostaglandin which causes uterine contractions in the bitch.

## Why does he try to escape the tie? He doesn't!

Most of us have watched dogs engage in breeding activity. Have you ever wondered why the stud dog begins to pull away from the bitch almost as soon as he lifts his leg and dismounts her? He sort of hunches his back and then pulls against her. I used to view it as an attempt by the dog to get away from the bitch, to be done with the breeding. Nothing, however, could be further from the truth. He is doing what he does because instinct has set up him to do it. His job is to get his sperm up the birth canal, through the cervix and all the way to the fallopian tubes before he departs from the bitch and goes on his way.

Mother Nature has designed the bitch and her reproduction system to interlock not only anatomically during the tie, but to also interlock in purpose. Any movement in the vagina at the time of breeding (and again during whelping) will set up uterine contractibility. Uterine contractibility does not work to expel something from the uterus, not even during whelping. Rather, contractions lift and pull the uterus upward in waves that will pull sperm upstream toward the eggs. He pulls; she contracts. Later when the bitch whelps, her uterine contractions will pull the uterus upward so that the cervix is slowly pulled back from the puppies as the fundus of the uterus exerts a downward push. Those contractions can be facilitated by feathering the vaginal wall. Those of us who have worked in labor/delivery have seen how that contracting uterus changes position within the abdomen of the mother as it lifts upwards toward her head and we have felt how the cervix pulls itself upward sort of like pulling a t-shirt over the baby's head. It provides the upward mobility necessary to pull sperm upward toward the eggs.

When the bitch is in a tie, her hormones are at the ready to facilitate this uterine action to insure that sperm is propelled rapidly toward her eggs. Each time the stud dog pulls against the bitch, he is setting up a wave of uterine contractions that are rapidly pulling the swimming sperm up toward the eggs. The vaginal ring clasps the bulb and holds it firmly in place as he pulls against her. When the job is done, the contractibility decreases and his bulb shrinks until finally when he pulls, he is released from the tie. The tie is an important part of the canine reproduction picture; insuring that the stud dog has a good chance of siring the litter by facilitating the actual penetration of the egg by his individual sperm during the tie. Time, prostaglandin and the creation of contractions have all worked together.

## Facilitating contractions after AI

Now you can clearly see why it is necessary to "mimic" the effects of the tie when doing an AI. It is easy to do, but it takes time. Once the AI rod is withdrawn, immediately begin a periodic stimulation of the vulva and vaginal tissues. Sometimes just applying intermittent pressure to the vulva is quite enough. Sometimes you will need to glove up with a sterile glove and enter the vagina with a gloved finger to feather the vaginal tissues intermittently to stimulate contractibility. There are two keys to success. First, the stimulation must be intermittent; not constant. The stud dog does not pull against the bitch constantly. He pulls intermittently allowing time between pulls for the contractions to begin, to build and to end. You must do the same. You will need to allow enough time to do the intermittent stimulations for at least fifteen to twenty minutes. Do not bother holding the bitch up by her back feet. This sounds fine until you recognize that in nature it does not happen and good luck on holding up the back feet of a Mastiff! Instead, allow the bitch to remain standing while you stimulate the vulva or the vaginal tissues every two to three minutes. Her body is designed to do this work in nature. You just need to provide the element that is missing.

If you stimulate the bitch's vaginal tissues following an AI, you will see your success rate rise and you will be as close to approximating the successes of natural breeding as possible. Our stud dogs do not breast feed and they do not regurgitate for their young. They are not monogamous as many canines are. However, they make an extremely important and vital contribution to each breeding with the tie. It *is* important.

# Chapter 6
# Who Are You Calling a Bitch?

## Our Much Beloved Girls

The reproductive system of the bitch is one of the more complex systems that we have an opportunity to watch in nature. First off, the bitch usually only comes into season once or twice a year versus many other mammals who come into season every 21-28 days or so. Next, she has two rather prominent uterine horns, which can be quite lengthy and reach well up into her body. Beyond that, the canine egg ovulates in an immature stage and ripens while free floating. Add in the wonders of the tie (see Chapter 5), which has a number of functions, but is very rare in the mammalian world, and you can easily see that the reproductive system of a bitch is a wonder of nature that can present challenges to the average dog breeder.

There was a time in our not too distant past when breeding dogs was easy. We left it in the their paws and let them do what they needed to do. With the advent of chilled and frozen sperm and the shipping of our bitches from coast to coast, breeding dogs has changed. The process has become more sophisticated and more dependent upon the breeder to understand the science of the reproductive system.

Clearly it is not as easy as it used to be. Dog breeders need to be a combination of animal lover and advocate, pooper-scooper, groomer, driver, showman and scientist. So many dog breeders do their jobs so well that I am constantly in awe of their inventiveness and willingness to do just about anything in order to succeed in their goals. If ever there was a group deserving of our respect and admiration, it is the individual who shows dogs and breeds them with an eye toward their good health as well as beauty.

A few years back, if a dog breeder wanted puppies they simply put Queenie or Fluffy in the back yard with Fido or Spot and let nature take its course. (Now it is more likely to be Tiffany or Elizabeth bred to Winston or Brad, but that is a completely different topic.) The breeder knew that timing was critical, but as long as Fido did his job and Fluffy did not object, you generally got puppies. If Fido did not perform, you just called in Spot to pinch hit and still got puppies. Dog breeders were not faced with pesky DNA testing of their stud dogs and if one boy did not get into the game, it was pretty easy to find another player.

After the introduction of frozen sperm, chilled sperm, easy air travel and DNA testing of stud dogs (and in some breeds, DNA testing of bitches as well), things became even more dependent on timing. Breeders have had to become more knowledgeable about science, as well as having to learn how to utilize sperm collection and AI in order to get our bitches in whelp. We have, for the most part, taken breeding out of their paws and placed it into our own paws, but we do not always get the job done as efficiently as did Fido and Fluffy. It is not that we cannot get the job done—it is that we have to work a bit harder than in times gone by. Let's have a conversation about the reproduction system of the bitch and see if we can get the details nailed down. Let's define our goals: puppies from the bitch we choose, sired by the stud dog we choose, in a time frame we know and in a method that provides as much safety as possible to mom and babies. Big order. Let's get started.

The bitch will come into her first season any time after five months of age. Toy dogs tend to come into season relatively young, larger dogs as late as two years of age. She will have her first season when she reaches about 85% of her adult size. This little indicator is very useful for those of us who run on bitches we have produced. (It is the same for the dogs. They begin sperm production when they reach about 85% of their adult size as well.) I am sure there are exceptions, but for most canines you will be able to count on that 85% rule.

When the bitch comes into her first season, you will usually see blood and sometimes quite a lot of it. She has not yet learned how to keep herself clean. It will advance through stages of color from red to pinkish and straw colored. This is a new experience for her. Her hormones may make her feel different. She may exhibit moodiness at first or become argumentative with the other girls when she is in season. This usually settles after a season or two and indeed some girls never exhibit any signs of behavioral changes. You can find any number of books and articles out there that go into more detail and use all of the scientific terms for what is happening in her body, but I write for dog breeders and so usually condense the information into the parts that dog breeders really need to know in order to reach our defined goals.

The bitch is now on her way toward ovulation. The two main hormones that impact ovulation that we can measure and need to track are progesterone and estrogen. There are other hormones too, of course, but they are measurable only with daily blood tests. That can get expensive for a dog breeder, so we are going to confine our conversation to just the two. These hormones are paving the way for ovulation—the eventual release of eggs from her ovaries. Along with emotional changes such as moodiness and irritation, she will exhibit behavior changes such as allowing other bitches in the kennel to mount her and as ovulation draws even closer, she will begin to mount other bitches. She will not allow dogs to mount her during this time. She is not fully *cornified* and she realizes it instinctively.

## Cornification

The bitch will also experience an important change within her vagina as she approaches ovulation. The cells that normally line the vaginal canal are a type of skin cells that are somewhat delicate. As she approaches ovulation and time for breeding, the cells that line the vagina change into a different type of skin cell that is more able to withstand the rigors of having the penis thrusting within the vagina. The cells inside the vagina become "cornified," thus giving her tender vaginal tissues some measure of protection against tearing and bruising. Viewing these cells with a microscope gives veterinarians valuable information about the bitch and where she is in her season. Cornification is not a good stand-alone test to know when the bitch is ready for breeding, but it can be a less expensive alternative to repeated progesterone testing. When used in combination with progesterone testing, the vaginal swab that allows a vet to see cornification of the cells lining the vagina can be useful.

## Progesterone levels

When the progesterone reaches the level of five ng/ml, give or take a point or two, the bitch ovulates. A bitch will ovulate anytime from day five after the first signs of her season all the way up to day twenty-one after the first signs of her season. The most common day is day ten. Obviously, her progesterone level may increase rather rapidly or creep up quite slowly. One thing that is for sure is that once she ovulates, the progesterone level will skyrocket. When her progesterone level reaches five ng/ml, she will no longer exhibit that slow, steady increase that blood tests show us. It will raise straight up and do it quickly.

Progesterone levels appear to be poorly understood. Many vets are encouraging breeders to base their breeding dates on the level that progesterone reaches after ovulation. While the majority of bitches may end up hovering around between twenty and 25 at the time of breeding, some of them may never go above ten and some will go as high as 70. Do not base your times for breeding on progesterone levels. It is a surefire way to fail. Instead, base your breedings on the age of the egg. That's right. I disagree with many of your vets. Once your bitch has ovulated, do not pay for further progesterone tests to determine the correct time to breed her. *Base breeding dates on the age of the egg and nothing else.*

Your goal is to determine which day your bitch ovulates. You can do this with progesterone testing combined with the knowledge that once a bitch ovulates, her progesterone level will take off like a rocket. If you get back a level of 5.4, for instance, you can assume she ovulated in the office while you waited for the blood draw. Even a level of 6 and 7 should be an indication to you that ovulation has recently occurred. It may take them anything from five to twenty-one days to reach the progesterone level of 5 ng/ml, but once that level has been reached, the progesterone level will rise very, very quickly.

Once you determine the date of ovulation (which you count as day one), you can add 62 more days to that date and have a good estimate of the whelping date. Very large litters for your breed might deliver a day or two sooner and singletons might deliver a day or two later, but normal sized litters will all deliver on day 63 unless there are unseen complications.

## The Fertile Focus

Another method you can use to determine date of ovulation is by tracking estrogen levels using a very handy and inexpensive little tool called a Fertile Focus. This device was designed for human use, but it can be easily adaptable to

the canine. I sell a lot of them and breeders have been very happy with them. The timing for its use is slightly different from when humans use it, but I can teach you how to use it and you will be pleased to have such an inexpensive and non-invasive little test for home use.

*The Fertile Focus.*

The Fertile Focus uses saliva from your bitch to determine the day that her estrogen level peaks. While progesterone levels rise steadily over a period of several days, the estrogen level rises to a quick, one day peak. By checking saliva of your bitch in season every morning, you can easily see the one day rise in estrogen. (I have included a very useful little graph that will explain the numbers.) The hardest part of the whole thing is getting the saliva from the bitch. If you are a Newfie breeder, you just wait for a drop of saliva and catch it as it falls. If you are a Chihuahua breeder, you will need to work a bit harder. Saliva tends to gather in the little pocket between the cheek and the gum. You only need enough saliva to make a little drop with some thickness to it. A lick will not do.

*Fertile Focus inner lens.*

Once you have the drop of saliva on the inner lens, put it aside and let it dry for 30 minutes. Reassemble the apparatus and, using the focus on the eyepiece, focus it until you can see the contents of the inner lens clearly. Be sure to keep pushing the little black button to keep the light source on. On the first day that her estrogen level rises, the saliva will "fern." It will show a very distinct pattern that has the appearance of a Boston fern. To me, it looks like ice that crystallizes on your windshield on icy mornings. Mark this day on your calendar and exactly five days from that date, your bitch will ovulate. Count that first day of "ferning" as day one. For instance, if you see full ferning on Monday, by counting Monday as day one, Tuesday as day two, etc., you know your bitch will ovulate on Friday.

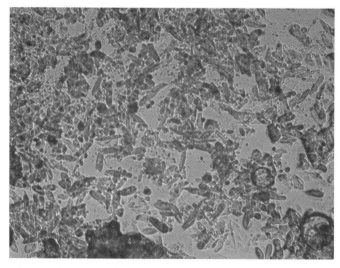

*Ferning salvia under the microscope.*

If you are planning an insemination using chilled or frozen sperm, you will need to nail down that timing even closer, so after seeing the full ferning of the sample, you can begin your progesterone tests. What follows is a list the various things you will need to do in order to use your Fertile Focus. The list will make for easy reference when you are ready:

- Check the saliva of your bitch every morning from the first sign of blood.

- Check the saliva each morning before you feed her or water her. (This is called NPO.)

- Use enough saliva to get a thick drop, but the drop can be very small.

- Remove the eyepiece from the apparatus by gently rocking it back and forth.

- Put the saliva on the inner lens of the eyepiece. See photos.

- Let the saliva drop dry on the inner lens for 30 full minutes.

- Reassemble the apparatus.

- Your bitch will ovulate five days after you see a "ferned" field.

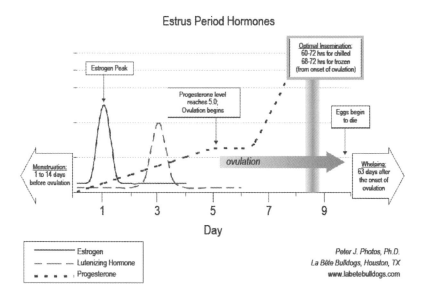

Estrus Period Hormones

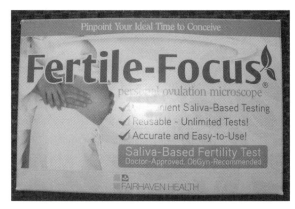

## Life span of the egg

I believe almost all dog breeders are familiar with the fact that the canine egg has a life span of five days. Most beginning dog breeders have discussed this with a vet or a friend who also breeds dogs. However, there is much more to the life span than you may have previously realized, so I would like to break it down for you day by day. You need to be able to comprehend completely and in detail what happens to the egg on each day of its life span, and then combine that knowledge with what you have learned about the life span of the sperm to be able to maximize your success in breeding, whether you use fresh, chilled or frozen sperm. When you are using chilled sperm with its life span of twelve hours and frozen sperm with its life span of one to two hours, you can no longer afford the luxury of discussing the life span of the eggs in 24-hour terms. You have to break it down into hourly increments.

- **Day one.** The egg has been ovulated and is in an immature state. Sperm cannot penetrate it even though it was deposited days ago. The sperm are just waiting and can do nothing to the egg at this point.

- **Day two.** Basically the same as day one. The egg is maturing, but the sperm cannot penetrate it.

- **Day three.** This is a day of intense interest. The egg becomes mature enough for penetration this day, but not at the beginning of the day. There is a big difference between an egg that is 49 hours old (beginning of day three) versus an egg that is 72 hours old (end of day three). The egg actually reaches maturation at approximately 60-68 hours of age. At that point, sperm can penetrate it and fertilization will occur. Just remember, the egg becomes fully mature at 60-68 hours of age.

- **Day four.** The eggs are all mature now and can be penetrated.

- **Day five.** The eggs are ripe and dying.

When we compare the life span of sperm and the life span of eggs, it is easy to know exactly how to time your breedings to maximize your success. With a minimum life span of five days, you can see how fresh sperm is the most versatile. Whether it is a natural breeding or an AI, fresh sperm allows you to place it even a day or two prior to ovulation and still have nice big litters. The sperm will easily live long enough to allow maturation of the eggs. They aren't just meandering meaninglessly about in the uterus if they arrive early. They are in the Fallopian tubes saving their energy and waiting. Using chilled sperm still gives you litters, but the timing becomes more critical. You will need to plan those breedings at the very end of the third day or anytime on day four to make sure you end up with puppies. Bringing frozen sperm into the equation makes timing even more critical. Now you will need to think in terms of hours; not days. Since frozen sperm have a life of only one to two hours, you will need to plan those breedings for the very last few hours of the third day or all day on day four. Do not let anyone talk you into using chilled or frozen sperm at the very beginning of day three. The sperm will be dead by the time the eggs can be penetrated.

Ultimately, success as a dog breeder rests on your shoulders. You are the one who is responsible for being a good steward of all of your resources including dog, bitch, sperm, egg, money, supplies and everything else that you use in the process of caring for your dogs. Insist on timing that you know to be appropriate. Do not let yourself be talked into procedures that do not fit within the framework of the life spans that we have discussed. The result will be missed breedings, small litters or singletons. I want you to succeed.

# CHAPTER 7

# DELIVERY TIME

### Free Whelp? C-section? What to Do?

This chapter is a difficult one to write because the subject of free whelping versus C-section is something of a hot button in the dog community. Everybody wants to weigh in on the issue from dog breeders to vets and everyone in between, including those of us who write books. It is a hot button in the human medical community too. The topic of C-sections is an important, but sensitive subject because on the one hand, everyone is of the opinion that C-sections save lives of babies and moms in real medical emergencies, but on the other hand, it should also be recognized that C-sections contribute to increased death rates for both moms and babies far more than vaginal deliveries do. Many breeders are under the mistaken impression that C-sections are "safer" for mom as well as her puppies. This is not true under any circumstances. Even in human situations, where the conditions are usually considerably better (better prenatal care, more staff, lengthier staff training and more equipment), the death rates for infants born by planned, elective (voluntarily done for no medical reason), C-sections is 1.77 deaths per 1000 births. Vaginal deliveries have a fetal death rate of 0.62 deaths per 1000 births. Safer? Not when almost three times as many babies die in planned C-sections as in vaginal deliveries. These statistics are not for the emergency C-sections when somebody is already at risk. These statistics are for the moms who walk into the hospital for a C-section long planned and anticipated. If you think that your vet's statistics are better, you are wrong.

## "C" stands for culprit

The human maternal death rate in the United States is on the rise. Shocking isn't it? Thirty years ago, the maternal death rate in humans was ten maternal deaths for every 100,000 live births. In 2004, the latest year for which statistics are available, the maternal death rate was 13.1 maternal deaths for every 100,000 live births. This is rather surprising considering that 90% of delivering moms have reasonably good health care and our OB physicians are trained well in their area of specialty. So what is contributing to the increased maternal death rate for human moms in our country? *C-sections.* In fact, "C" should stand for Culprit. C-sections have become so common that many people refer to them as "C-births" or even "C's." It's sort of pathetic when you cozy up to a surgical procedure to such an extent that you give it a nick name. Pet names aside, it is clear that everyone involved has lost sight of the fact that a C-section is major abdominal surgery with significantly increased risks to both moms and babies. The risk of bleeding and infection is always present. C-sections are inherently riskier for both mom and baby than vaginal deliveries. If it were not so, Mother Nature would have designed us all with zippers.

If more human moms are dying because of their C-sections, how can you possibly think that more canine moms are *not* dying as a result of theirs? Canine moms are indeed dying because of C-sections and they are often taking their entire litters with them. Does this mean that no breeder should ever consider having a C-section on a bitch? No, it does not. Does it mean that no vet should ever perform a C-section on a bitch? No, it does not mean that either. What it means is that vets and breeders alike should stop viewing planned C-sections as a safer means of delivery. Heaven forbid that it should ever be viewed as a tool of convenience. C-sections need to be put back on the shelf for use during emergencies when x-rays and vaginal exams of the bitch have demonstrated a medical indication for major abdominal surgery. Planning C-sections under the guise of being safer for mom and babies is just plain wrong. It just is not so for humans and it isn't so for dogs.

The maternal death rate in bitches during or shortly after a C-section is somewhere in the neighborhood of 1% overall and significantly higher in some breeds. This is an outrageous number. As high as the human death rate is climbing, it does not come near one maternal death for every 100 C-sections. If one out of every 100 C-sections moms were dying in the human community, people would be screaming for improvement. Physicians would stop offering elective C-sections to their patients and their patients would stop asking for them. Major surgeries would be saved only for times when mom or baby is at risk. C-sections should not be done as often on humans as they are being done currently and they should not be done as often as they are being done on bitches. Our bitches are dying during C-sections at an alarming rate.

Where is the outrage? Well, it's right here for starters. I am outraged at the number of C-sections being performed on bitches and I am appalled at the number of litters that are dying during C-sections. I am, quite literally, horrified to hear and read of the large numbers of "planned" C-sections that are being done on our girls. I am mortified to hear about the numbers of bitches who have undergone dangerous surgery simply because two or three hours have passed since the last puppy was whelped. I'm angry that many of those decisions are based on the poorly informed use of fetal monitors designed for humans (one uterus, one infant) and now being used on dogs (two uterine horns and multiple infants). Later in this chapter, I will give you a lot of information about fetal monitoring. I hope that it will help somebody somewhere and keep a bitch from having to undergo an unnecessary surgery. It upsets me to think of the number of dog breeders who have had to face the death of their bitch because of a C-section. Keep it up, and in a hundred years or so, our dogs will have completely lost the ability to free whelp. Is that the future you want for dogs? Really?

Recently, I gave a seminar to a group of Clumber Spaniel breeders. There were only about twenty-five breeders present at the seminar. In that small group, four breeders had lost Clumber girls during C-sections. Imagine that. Four out of twenty-five breeders or so had undergone the horrifying experience of watching their bitch die. I get hundreds of emails a month, and quite a few of them are about C-sections, loss of moms and loss of litters. I do not want dog breeders to have to go through the guilt and the grief that accompanies the unnecessary death of a much loved bitch. That is why I am writing this chapter. What is happening? Why is it happening? What is normal and what is abnormal during the birth process of the bitch? What can we do to avoid C-sections? Let's take a look at each of these questions one by one.

## What is happening?

What is happening is that the C-section rate for dogs is climbing right alongside the C-section rate for humans. In dogs, the C-section rate is sitting somewhere around 33 to 35%, and is as much as 100% in some breeds and with some breeders. It is roughly the same as for humans. As the C-section rate climbs, the death rate is climbing as well for moms and puppies. Some of those litters are taken from the womb days before they are due and the entire litter is born dead—premature puppies who never lived to take a breath. Nobody is trying to do the wrong thing. Nobody is being careless or negligent; everybody is trying to do the right thing. But in spite of his or her best intentions, the wrong thing is done. The wrong choices are made and your dogs are paying the price. Eventually the species will pay the price.

## Why is it happening?

What seems to be happening is that everybody is afraid. Breeders are afraid of losing their bitches and puppies if they do not do C-sections. Vets are afraid of the loss of bitches and puppies during vaginal deliveries at home and they appear to be very uneasy about making the wrong decision when the question is to cut or not to cut. Nobody wants to be wrong, and nobody wants to be the responsible party when the wrong decision is made. It isn't really any different in the human medical community. Nobody wants to be responsible for making the wrong decision. Every decision made is made by a desire to cover your own bases at the moment rather than worry about the end result. Who is to blame? Nobody. Nobody is to blame, but everybody needs to sit back, gather some sensible data, and get their priorities straight. Everybody from the breeder to the vet needs to re-group and attack this thing from the angle of knowledge and information instead of the angle of fear.

Once again, we need to recognize that Mother Nature is our friend when it comes to all things to do with reproduction—and we all too often are treating her like an enemy who is never invited to the party. A little bit of information on the topic of whelping may end up saving the life of your girl. My information comes primarily from meeting and talking to hundreds of breeders every year. It comes from my own experiences with dog breeding; my own fears about whelping, my own guilt and my past C-section rate. I also have a considerable amount of information gathered during the many years I worked as a labor/delivery RN spending hundreds of hours in the delivery room. I do as much reading and research as I can. First on the agenda, is to share with you important information about fetal monitors and how they work.

## Fetal monitoring tutorial

I will start off by giving you a written source that you can check if you wish. The book that most of us use when taking fetal monitoring classes is called *Fetal Heart Monitoring Principles and Practice,* distributed by AWHONN and written by Feinstein, Torgersen, and Atterbury, published by Kendall/Hunt. This is a book written about human fetal monitoring. There are no books about canine fetal monitoring. I can, however, teach you about fetal monitoring for humans. However, I believe that once you understand how it really works, you will understand why it has such a limited application in the canine.

Fetal monitoring has two components, the most important of which of course is the monitoring of the fetus. Although it is a heartbeat that we monitor, fetal monitoring is *not* about fetal hearts. What we are monitoring is the central nervous system of the fetus. Essentially, what is being monitored is what his brain does. The less important component is the monitoring of the uterine contractions. The primary reason for monitoring uterine contractions is to determine the relationship between the contraction and the baby's brain. *This is the reason that Dopplers do not give us valuable information.* The Doppler can be used only randomly, not constantly. In order for us to see the most valuable part, we must be able to monitor the heart of the fetus continually—before, during and after a contraction.

The use of an external monitor over the abdomen of the mother or the bitch cannot, no exceptions to this rule, determine the strength of a contraction. On a monitor strip, the contraction can be so tall as to be off the graph paper or it can look like an ant hill, but no matter what you "see" on the strip, *the strength of the contraction cannot be determined by an external monitor or a device that lies on the abdomen of the mother.* In a labor/delivery setting if the medical staff needs to know the strength of a contraction, the doctor would rupture the bag of water and the nurse would thread an internal pressure catheter up behind the baby. With an external monitor that sits on the abdomen, you can learn only one fact—the timing of the contractions. You can see when one begins, how long it lasts, and when it stops. Braxton Hicks contractions, false contractions, premature contractions, pushing contractions; all look the same.

To reiterate: No one can determine the strength of contractions by looking at a monitor strip if an external monitor is used. Mom can be sound asleep with contraction patterns that look like mountains, or she can be delivering her baby with contraction patterns that look like anthills. *There are no exceptions to this rule.*

## Why doesn't my vet know more about fetal monitoring?

Vets simply have no way of learning fetal monitoring. For medical doctors, it is taught in classrooms where strips are studied, followed by hands-on experience sitting at the bedsides of laboring human mothers. Certified Fetal Monitor Instructors teach it. Following the classroom experience, they learn more from the experience of working with the monitors daily in their careers. A veterinarian, by contrast, simply has no way of gaining access to the bedsides of laboring mothers. They are forced to get their information from the people who rent the monitors and, judging by the numbers of dead and premature puppies, being delivered on the say so of a telephone diagnosis since the companies renting the equipment do not know fetal monitoring themselves. There is no excuse for diagnosing true labor via a phone call. The best OB doc in the world still needs a vaginal exam to feel dilation of the cervix. When I asked one of the companies a few questions, the one response I got was that their "maternal death rate" was zero. This was most unimpressive because fetal monitoring is just that—*fetal*. There is no way to change the outcome, nor determine a danger to the mother by fetal monitoring. Not for humans, and not for dogs.

Here is a little review of this section:

1. It is the brain of the fetus we are monitoring, not the cardiac function.

2. It is *impossible* to determine the strength of the uterine contraction by the placement and reading of an external monitor.

3. The most important component of fetal monitoring is monitoring the response of the fetal brain to the maternal contraction; the relationship between contraction and fetal brain.

4. Dopplers cannot determine fetal distress. (Dopplers are rarely used in labor/delivery anymore. It's old technology in that department. I probably used one five to six times in 25 years.)

5. Vets have no way to learn fetal monitoring in the setting for which it was invented and intended. Accept going in that they know nothing about fetal monitoring. How could they have learned it? What human hospital is going to allow vets at the bedsides of laboring women?

6. Maternal health and outcomes cannot be determined by fetal monitoring. The only individuals I have ever heard even hint at that claim were the people who rent fetal monitoring equipment to dog breeders. Physicians and nurses who work in Labor/Delivery day in and day out for their entire careers know that fetal monitoring is all about the fetus.

## External fetal monitoring of uterine contractions

Human anatomy varies considerably from that of a canine, but one of the more critical differences lies in the fact that a woman has two nipples, both well above her abdomen. The bitch has several nipples and they lie along the entire length of her abdomen. *This* is a very critical and important thing to remember when discussing fetal monitoring and why the information gathered on a bitch can be so inaccurate.

There are two types of tests that Labor and Delivery nurses are asked to do for pregnant patients on an almost daily basis. One is called a Non-Stress Test. The other is called a Stress Test. The stress we are talking about is the stress caused by a uterine contraction. In a Non-Stress Test, the mother is hooked up to the fetal monitor for 30 minutes to an hour and the strip is read and interpreted by the nurse, with results called into the doctor. All it does is look at what the baby is doing at the moment. Is he sleeping? If so, what does his resting heart rate look like? Is he moving around? If so, what does movement do to his heart rate, which increases its rate as directed by the brain.

The Stress Test involves initiating contractions, running the test for twenty to 30 minutes or so, interpreting the test results and calling them into the doctor. At that point, the doctor will decide if intervention is needed. He will base his decision on what happens to the baby's brain before, during and after a contraction—contractions the nurse has started. How do we initiate contractions on a woman who is not in labor? *Easy!!* By stimulating her nipples. We can often get a good uterine contraction pattern going by simply flicking her nipples or asking her to rub them gently. Oftentimes, all she has to do is apply pressure to the nipple, even a single nipple. That simple action will start uterine contractions.

So what are the implications here for the monitoring of the contractions of a bitch? How about the implications for a bitch with a wide belt wrapped around her abdomen and in constant contact with her nipples? How about how often the nipples are flicked during the placement of the belt and the pressure of the belt upon the nipples? Contractions can be started by the merest touch on nipples. It means that each and every time the belt is placed on the bitch's abdomen, you are at risk for starting uterine contractions, which to the laymen's eye (or ear I suppose, considering the diagnosis is made by telephone) would indicate labor. Is it labor? No. Will it result in delivery of the puppies? No. Can the strength of those little contractions be determined by the "look" on the strip of an external monitor? *No, No, No, a thousand times No!*

There is a type of contraction called a Braxton Hicks contraction. Braxton Hicks contractions are nothing more than little "tune-up" contractions. They may be responsible for moving the baby into position, or a form of mild exercise for the uterus. This contraction looks like a normal contraction on a monitor. They become more frequent as the gestation progresses. Do bitches have Braxton Hicks contractions? Yes, they do along with cattle, horses and humans. I have certainly felt contractions on my bitches even two weeks before time for delivery. I have also initiated them by minimal nipple stimulation. How long do they last? They can last for hours or can be simply a handful of contractions. Braxton Hicks contractions are what we call "false labor." They look identical to the regular uterine contraction on a fetal monitor.

You cannot tell them apart. There is a simple way to tell if contractions are truly laboring contractions versus false labor: a simple exam of the cervix to determine dilation—hard to do over the phone, however.

The difference between Braxton Hicks contractions and true uterine contractions is that true uterine contractions will result in cervical changes and eventual delivery. Braxton Hicks contractions will result in nothing. Eventually they will go away, only to return another day, or more to the point, only to return the next time the nipples are stimulated by a wide belt around the abdomen and nipples. Can uterine contractions be initiated by the placement of a monitor belt placed on top of nipples? Yes. So, exactly how accurate does uterine monitoring look for a bitch? By now, I believe that most of you would agree that it is meaningless, even dangerous to the point of giving inaccurate information to people who have no training in fetal monitors.

Some additional points to remember:

1.  Fetal monitors were designed for human use, designed anatomically to avoid contact with human nipples.

2.  Even minimal nipple stimulation can set up a pattern of contractions.

3.  Contractions caused by nipple stimulation are false contractions, but because you cannot determine the strength of contractions from an external fetal monitor, the information is misleading, and leads to early C-sections with loss of entire litters. Is this happening? Yes, all over the United States. It is happening because fetal monitoring equipment cannot be used on the canine with success.

We have already figured out that external monitors do not give us much information about uterine contractions, but we also know that they do read out a pattern. What is it that they are sensing if not uterine contraction strength? They are sensing the skin tension. They are certainly able to sense when the tension of the skin changes, altered by the muscle under the skin contraction. They also give us an important piece of information—the timing of the contraction. They are as accurate as an internal pressure catheter at telling us when a contraction begins, how long it lasts and when it ends. That information is important, *but only in the context of how the fetal heart tones respond to the contraction.*

Your fingertips can detect the contractions without an electronic piece of equipment. You do not need a monitor to do that. You do need a monitor, however, to tell you how the fetal heart responds to the stress of a contraction. Can a Doppler tell you this? No. A Doppler picks up the heartbeat of a single fetus at a time and cannot give you a single piece of useful information other than the heart rate of one puppy. Fetal monitor components, when used together, give us important information about how the fetus is reacting to his environment. Remember when we discussed that fetal monitoring really does not have anything to do with the heart even though it is a heartbeat we are looking at?

What we want to see is the "reactivity" of the fetal heart. If the baby so much as moves his foot, we want to see his heart rate go up. If he is sleeping, we want to see a slower heart beat with little reactivity. In other words, we are looking for a sleep pattern. If the baby is doing somersaults in utero, we want to see the heart really racing in exactly the same way that your heart reacts when you run up a flight or two of stairs. The brain is the organ that tells the heart to speed up when it needs more oxygen, and it is brain activities that we are monitoring when we monitor the fetal heart. We want to see the baby's brain telling the heart how to react to its environment. A Doppler is simply incapable of doing that with its random fetal heart beat checks. Handy to read the fetal heart rate, but not very useful for anything else. We actually use Dopplers more for detecting blood flow through the arteries than we do to listen to fetal hearts. Dopplers have not been useful in OB for a long, long time. Medical-surgical nurses use them. For us, they are old science.

## Maternal heart rate versus fetal heart rate

One of the most common mistakes made is to listen to mom's heartbeat and assume it is that of the baby. This mistake is even more common when you are attempting to listen to a litter of heart beats while meantime, mom's aorta, femoral arteries, mammary arteries and all of her other arteries are pounding out a beat. Do you think that you would be incapable of making a mistake? Wrong. You are more than capable. How many puppies have you listened to that had heart rates in the 130 to150 range? That was probably the mom. Let me tell you a story, and if at the end of the story, you still don't think that you could make that common mistake, you'll have to do some convincing to make me a believer.

A few years back, a woman came into Emergency Room following a bad motor vehicle accident. Her car was hit head-on by a large truck. The woman was seven months pregnant at the time. All day long, the medical staff kept her in ER because her pelvis and both legs were fractured. They kept phoning up report to me because, of course, if she went into labor they would send her up to Labor and Delivery where I work. Through two shifts, one of the ER nurses would call me with reports like: Maternal heart rate, 116; Fetal HR, 120. Both ER docs also called me with reports. They were using nothing but a Doppler and everyone I spoke with resisted my offer of help. Finally, at about seven pm, the woman started into labor and they sent her up. ER staff does not manage obstetrical situations if there is an OB department within the facility. They do not waste their resources on OB when the OB department is just a short distance away. A Labor-Delivery RN is about as useless in ER as an ER nurse is in Labor-Delivery. We each have our area of expertise, and the two specialties do not intersect successfully.

When I got the patient, I found her heart rate easily. It was 120 beats per minute. She was in considerable pain because of her injuries and that undoubtedly accounted for her higher than normal heart rate. The fetal heart rate was zero. I could not find fetal heart. I turned the Ultrasound machine on and quickly saw that the baby's heart was not beating. He was dead. He had died in the automobile accident when the mom's pelvis was crushed. There was no doubt about it, the little baby boy had a crushed head on delivery. The ER staff had been picking up the maternal heart tones all day long and identifying them as fetal heart tones. If two ER docs and a variety of ER nurses can make that mistake, so can you. Trust me. It is a common mistake.

If you are listening regularly and you hear puppy heart tones that are consistently lower than normal, there is a good chance that you are hearing the mother. Even if you do hear fetal heart tones that are consistently lower than what is considered normal, do you know what that means? Exactly nothing. It means that the puppy has a lower heart rate. It is not an indication of fetal distress. It is meaningless information that will undoubtedly, in the hands of the wrong people, lead to a C-section. Consistently decreased fetal heart tones do not have meaning. It is the up and down pattern of the rate that means something, and only then when decreased heart tones are viewed in conjunction with the uterine contractions.

Do you suppose that when an OB doctor does an inappropriate C-section that he later runs into the patient's room and tells her that that, as it turned out, she didn't need a C-section? No. He goes in, tells her it was touch and go and that she is lucky that he moved as fast as he did. Do you think your vet will do differently? He or she will not. They will tell you the same thing the OB doc who sectioned without a reasonable cause—it was touch and go, those pups looked iffy and you are lucky that he got them out when he did. Medical people do not go looking for lawsuits or unhappy patients, and they count on the fact that the breeder does not know about whelping and is only looking for living puppies.

## Fetal distress: What it is, and what it is not

We have covered the fact that if a puppy's heart beat is consistently lower than the stated averages, it is not fetal distress, nor is it a sign of fetal distress. If it is the same lower rate at all times, it is simply that: a lower heart rate than usual. Although we considered the range of 140-160 to be the normal heart rate for a human fetus, if we got a baby in who was running consistently lower or higher, it was not cause for alarm. I have watched babies who ran in the 110-120 range and also babies who were running in the 160-170 range. It is not the heart beat rate that we are looking at on the monitor. Remember? It is the reactivity of the fetal heart to its environment. If the baby was moving, did its heart rate increase? If so, we considered it a reactive heart (it reacted to what its brain told it to do) and left well enough alone.

There was one slight contradiction to that. If, over the several hours that the mother was in labor, the baby's base rate slowly *increased,* it was a sign of maternal and or fetal fever. We would often see this in Beta Strep babies. We didn't prepare for a C-section, but we watched everything carefully and the doc treated mom, both for infection and fever.

Listening by Doppler gave us only the baby's heart rate. It did not give us the piece of information we were after, right? So what it is that we needed to see in order for the doc to diagnosis fetal distress and do an emergency C-section? Before I answer that important question, let me first describe the three basic types of deceleration of fetal heart beats. The first two, although very dramatic looking on the strip and dramatic sounding on the monitor are benign, harmless and unremarkable.

## Variable decelerations of the fetal heart

Anytime pressure is put on the umbilical cord during the laboring or delivery process, there will be a very rapid and extremely dramatic deceleration of the fetal heart tones. These are called variable decelerations because they occur randomly without any pattern. It is almost as if the kid is in there squeezing his cord for fun. They come and go. They are, however, very dramatic and quite frightening if you do not know what they are. The sound that the heart tones make can go from 160 to twenty in a matter of seconds, and then right back up to 160 again equally as fast. If the cord is caught between two hard surfaces for a few seconds, you will hear the variable decelerations of fetal heart tones. Is this a reason for a C-section? Not normally for human deliveries, and certainly never for a canine.

If the variable decels became more frequent as the human baby's head comes down into the pelvic area, then a C-section would be considered because there is always the chance that the cord was wrapped around the neck enough times and tightly enough that the baby simply wasn't going to be able to make it all the way out. He would be held in place by the shortened length of his cord. How common is it for the cord to be around the baby's neck? Very common. Maybe as often as half the time, but it does not usually cause problems. How often do you see it in a puppy delivery? Probably never. However, if a vet happened to be listening with a Doppler to the right puppy at the right time, and heard that very dramatic decrease in fetal heart tones, chances are good that you would be looking at a C-section. So remember: Deep dramatic decels? Cord compression. Change mom's position, take her for a walk to shake things around a little, hydrate her very well and forget that you heard it.

## Early decelerations of the fetal heart tones

Head compression causes decelerations of fetal heart tones. This is normal, natural and is, in fact, the sign of a good, reactive brain. Early decels "mirror" the contraction. As the reading for the contraction begins, the fetal heart begins to decrease in rate. The higher the read out on the contraction goes (picking up skin tension, remember) the lower the read out for the fetal heart goes. It will be the puppy who is coming through the cervix that will be having early decelerations of fetal heart tones. Tell me how you can see that mirroring pattern by the use of a Doppler? You cannot. Early decels, which simply mirror the pattern of the contraction, are normal and natural. They are, in fact a sign of a good, reactive brain. Can you hear the decrease of the fetal heart with a Doppler? Yes. Can you see that it is a harmless, benign pattern with a Doppler? No. Will a vet section your bitch if he hears those fetal heart tones going down into the 50's and 60's? Yes, many of them will. Will he assume that he is hearing fetal distress? You bet he will. Will the puppies come out looking half dead? Sure. That is often one of the by-products of the anesthesia. Unless the vet is really, really fast in his surgery techniques, those pups are going to get a big dose of anesthetic. Did it have anything at all to do with fetal distress? No, in all likelihood it did not.

## Late decelerations of fetal heart tones

Now we are going to talk about genuine fetal distress. Even though a fetal monitor often demonstrates genuine distress, the majority of these babies (the human kind) come out pink and screaming. What looks awful on the monitor and simply cannot be ignored by a good OB doctor, however, is usually not as dramatic as it looked on the monitor. This is why I tell people repeatedly that all human fetal monitoring has accomplished is a higher C-section rate, which has led to a higher death rate. This is a simple fact. Docs simply must perform a C-section for late decelerations (late decals) because the doc cannot tell if the baby is in true distress or not. Legalities being what they are, when presented with late decels of fetal heart tones, a C-section must be done and done quickly. Occasionally, the baby is in bad shape on arrival, but most of the time, the kid looks fine in person, even though he looked crappy on the monitor. So, what are the implications of late decels?

Following the completion of a contraction, or right at the end of a contraction, you will see a very, very subtle (not deep and dramatic, and not deep enough to "mirror" a contraction) deceleration of heart tones. It is usually not a decrease of more than a few beats per minute. Again, the pattern these decels make is often times very subtle. These types of decels are never normal and natural, they are always bad, but luckily they are usually caught soon enough in the laboring process that the doc is able to get the baby out of there fast enough that no harm was done.

What do they mean? They mean that during the contraction, the placenta was squeezed with enough pressure that the blood supply to the baby was cut off or severely decreased. They are not cord compression, and they aren't head compression, they are a sign that the baby's brain was actually deoxygenated for a long enough period of time that it affected the heart and it actually slowed down due to lack of oxygen to the brain. Clearly, this is not a good thing. This is reason for a C-section and clearly, you are not able to "hear" this very subtle pattern with a Doppler. In fact, by the time the contraction has ended, you are not even going to be listening anymore and you certainly will not pick up a subtle decel with your ear alone. Late decels of fetal heart tones are the only decelerations that indicate fetal distress. Prolonged late decels over several hours of labor can cause severe brain damage.

## What are late decels?

- *Not* a consistently lowered heart rate.

- *Not* a deep and dramatic decrease that happens randomly.

- *Not* a deep, mirroring of the contraction.

Fetal distress is indicated when the fetal heart tones decrease in a subtle manner following or near the end of the contraction. Late decels are threatening, the other two types are not.

## A summarized list of what has been covered:

1. External monitoring devices *cannot* detect the strength of a uterine contraction. It senses the tension in the skin and registers that and that alone.

2. You can stimulate uterine contractions in your bitch simply by attaching the fetal monitor belt. They can last as long as the belt is in contact with the nipples, or can go away quickly. These contractions are *not* laboring contractions. You caused them yourself by attaching the belt over the nipples. This is one more reason why the technology is not appropriate for canines.

3. Monitoring devices are for a human woman with one uterus, one fetus and no nipples on her abdomen. (If a woman has nipples on her abdomen, she has many issues other than pregnancy anyhow.)

4. A Doppler can only give you a current fetal heart rate. It is impossible to detect fetal distress with a Doppler.

5. Even professionals often mistake mom's heart rate for baby's when using a Doppler.

6. A consistently lower heart rate, as long as it is reactive, is not a sign of anything but a lower heart rate.

7. You know now what a variable decel is. You know what causes it and you know it is benign most of the time for a human and *always* for a canine.

8. You know what an early decel is. You know what causes it and you know it is benign.

9. You know what a late decel is. You know it can well be deadly and you know why: Deprive the brain of oxygen often enough and long enough and you will end up with brain damage.

10. You have, at least, been told the limitations of using human fetal monitors on bitches.

## Where is your true treasure?

What is the treasure within your kennel? It is your bitch. The girls in your kennel are your treasure and one of your most valued possessions. They are your priority. Our lovely girls gestate without complaint, whelp quietly and without complaint for the most part, and spend weeks gently caring for their babies. They spend hours on end licking their little bottoms and nursing. Although you have undoubtedly invested a lot of time and money in the breeding, and you have a tremendous amount of emotional investment in the unborn puppies, the bitch is, nevertheless, your treasure. So from now on, base your decisions on what is best for her. Ask yourself the question: "If I had to lose one or the other, would I choose to lose my bitch or one or even all of the puppies?" Make your whelping decisions based on the answer to that question and your bitch should win every time. The number of bitches who die in free whelps is so small and it happens so infrequently as to be almost inconsequential. Of course, the puppies are valuable to us in many ways, but they are also in fact, unknowns. You would be inconsolable if you decided to section your bitch to save a puppy and the bitch died. Your bitch is your pet, your loving companion and your treasure. Base your decisions on her health and well-being and you will be a better dog breeder as a result. You will be a good steward of your resources.

## How many bitches die while free whelping?

The answer is almost none. At every seminar, I ask the breeders present how many of them have owned, or know of a bitch, who has died in a free whelp. Over many years, I have talked to a total of just three breeders who lost bitches during free whelping. Those deaths appeared to be caused by cardiac events of some sort. Compare that to the four out of a single group of 25 who had lost bitches to C-sections. It is an extremely rare event for a bitch to die while free whelping just as it is an extremely rare event for a human mom to die in the middle of a vaginal delivery. I have never known of one in the human arena although I am sure it has happened. It didn't happen to any of the hundreds of women who were my labor/delivery patients. How many bitches have you personally owned or known that died in a free whelp? If you believe that the number of bitches who die while whelping is very, very small, and if you are convinced that your bitches are the treasure in your kennel, you are well on your way toward making the best possible decisions.

## How many puppies die during delivery?

Statistically, at least 30% of all puppies who are born end up dying either at birth or shortly after. If you breed dogs long enough, eventually you will have to deal with the death of some puppies. It is always sad and often quite devastating. If it happens enough, it will take a definite emotional toll on you.

I suspect that it is the death of puppies that leads eventually to the end of dog breeding endeavors for so many of us. That grief eventually begins to out-weigh the joys of breeding and many people give it up almost as an act of self-preservation. (It is nothing—absolutely nothing—compared to the feelings of losing a bitch during a C-section, so keep your priorities straight and it will help you to make good decisions in all circumstances.) Puppies get stuck during the whelping process and sometimes they are stuck for too long and simply can't be revived. Some puppies have unseen birth defects and end up being incompatible with life outside the womb. They do fine as long as their umbilical cords are connected through the placenta to mom's life-giving oxygen, but once they are on their own and independent they cannot survive. This happens occasionally with human babies as well. Are you willing to put mom's life at risk to save a puppy? A litter of puppies? Before you decide to do a C-section, really think carefully about those questions. There are going to be puppies that die in the period of time surrounding birth; bitches do not have to.

## What is a normal full-term whelping pattern?

There is no normal whelping pattern. The variations are endless just as it is with humans. It is certainly possible to discuss the generalities of whelping, but each bitch is different, each breed is different, and each delivery is different.

Bitches will usually deliver their litters just about 63 days after ovulation. A bitch with a larger than normal litter will deliver a day or two earlier and bitches with singletons will often deliver a little bit later. A bitch will usually refuse breakfast on the day she whelps. The *prodromal* (beginning) stage of labor will frequently last twelve hours or more. It is at this stage of labor during which the cervix effaces during uterine contractions and dilation begins. The contractions may occur every twenty minutes or so and may last for twenty to thirty seconds at the beginning. Your bitch is aware of the impending delivery of her puppies, but in the beginning, she may not show any outward signs. She may do some digging, and she may seem a bit agitated or restless. She will want you to be nearby. If you keep your hand on her tummy, you can definitely feel the contractions as her abdomen tightens.

She will have instinctively stopped eating, probably for two reasons. First, uterine contractions use up energy, so does intestinal peristalsis. She instinctively knows that, at this time, she needs to use her energy on the contractions necessary to efface and dilate her cervix. Later, she will use up lots of energy pushing out puppies. Not eating is normal and natural for most bitches, so do not worry about it. Make sure she has lots of water to drink during labor.

Some girls decide they are not going to drink water either. Try adding a little bit of goat's milk to the water, that will often encourage her to drink more. Some bitches will chow down while pushing out a puppy though, so you need to be aware that they are each different about eating while in labor.

Once labor is well established, she will probably become very clingy and not want you out of her sight. This too is normal, but it is important to note that if a bitch gives birth while you are not present, her instincts will kick in and she will usually do a good job without you. Remember these girls are filled to the brim with instinct. It is how the species has thrived for so many thousands of years. It takes several hours of labor to efface and then dilate the cervix. Once she has fully dilated, the second stage of labor begins. The contractions have also helped to push a puppy toward the cervix and once a puppy has entered into the cervix, her pushing action will begin. The presence of a puppy in the cervix will trigger her natural instincts to push, although her pushing may not be effective at the beginning.

*Oral Cal Plus.*

Her body will release oxytocin, which acts as a clock to say when the contractions start, how long they last and when they end. Her body also releases parathyroid hormone that acts like a key to unlock her bones and allow calcium to flow from her storage depots (bones) to the blood stream where it is carried to each individual muscle cell to effect a strong contraction. If you feel that more contractions are needed, you can walk her briskly or do a bit of nipple stimulation. If you feel that the contractions need to be stronger, feel free to give her calcium. I recommend using a product called Oral Cal Plus. You can also use Tums.

The contractions will continue to push the puppy through the cervix and the further into the birth canal the puppy gets, the more effective her pushes will be. It is the same for humans. This is the most painful time of the delivery for her and she may cry during the contractions at this time. Be comforting to her, but there is no reason for you to be fearful. If you have ever given birth—you need to remember that all of us felt like crying at that time, whether we did or not. It is the same for your bitch. If her crying alarms you and makes you fearful, she will probably sense that and become even more agitated.

Once the puppy has made it through the cervix and into the vagina, you will be able to see a bulge at her vulva. Once you see that bulge—you are home free. She will quickly deliver the puppy. Be watchful, but if you can—and I know how hard it is to do—let her handle the opening of the sac and the chewing of the cord. It is a very difficult thing to do because we are all so eager to grab the puppy and run with it, but the more mom does on her own, the stronger her parenting instincts will become and the better mother she will be. Let her be—even if you have to sit on your hands. Step in only if the puppy appears to be dead or if mom gets carried away with chewing of the cord. Be watchful, but try to allow mom to do what nature has prepared her to do. It will be to her benefit.

## Vanilla ice cream

One of the best breeder tips I was ever given came from several different dog breeders and it is such a wonderful tip that it deserves its own little section. The use of small amounts of vanilla ice cream between puppies is a lifesaver. The ice cream is primarily a fluid for a bitch that has probably refused to eat or drink, and glucose for the puppies who can definitely use a boost prior to delivery to facilitate their vigorous kicking and squirming within the birth canal. Do not forget that movement within the vagina creates contractibility at the time of the tie and at the time of whelping. Last, but certainly far from least, vanilla ice cream provides calcium for the mom to create strong contractions.

## Should the bitch eat her placentas?

Placentas are filled with blood. This blood, at the time of whelping, has a lot of calcium in it. Placental tissues are pure protein. Mother Nature has given your bitch the instinct not to eat the day of whelping in order to preserve her energies for whelping instead of digestion. Nature has also given her the instinct not to leave her babies behind when they are still newborns while she leaves the nest to hunt down food. Many breeders notice that their bitches will usually not appear interested in food the day or two following birth. These things all work together in a way that Nature intends them to work if we simply stop interfering. Allow her to eat as many placentas following whelping as she cares to eat. She will consume a rich protein source that contains a lot of calcium at a time when she needs calcium for strong contractions and calcium to produce milk. The pure protein in her placentas *is* her food source for the day or two following whelping. Don't tamper with the process and the end result will be good for your bitch and for her puppies.

## Watch your bitch—not the clock!

Now we enter into the big, gray area that is responsible for so many unneeded C-sections. I have no idea how the myth got started that a bitch needed to deliver a puppy every two hours or she is in trouble. I truly do not know who started it or why, but whoever it was, they were dead wrong. If I could have any wish granted, it would be that every dog breeder on the face of the planet toss out their clock the second their bitch goes into labor. I wish that breeders paid more attention to their bitches and less attention to their clock. Watch your bitch and stop watching your clock. Your bitch will "tell" you if she is in trouble. She will push over an hour with no progress, pace endless and squat repeatedly as though she is urinating. If she behaves in this manner for an hour, you need to see your vet for an x-ray to check puppy positions. Bitches deliver their puppies in a very random pattern. The majority of them deliver a puppy every 30 minutes to four hours, but many of them take as long as 24 hours to deliver their litter (sometimes even longer) and lengthy rest breaks between puppies are normal, natural and necessary.

Some breeds are very slow and lazy whelpers, but that is normal for them. How would you like to pump out a baby every hour? How do you suppose you would keep up with the cleaning, feeding and cord care of each baby? How tired do you suppose you might get if you push and push and then had only a brief break before you had to do it all over again, and again, and again? Doesn't it make sense that a bitch would have a few puppies, then take a break during which she can nap while her new babies get their first feeding, undisturbed by the onset of pushing out yet another sibling? Once mom has rested and the babies are well-fed, contractions can begin again and mom can care for new arrivals, knowing that the first-born puppies have been well fed and will be content while she cares for new ones.

Remember when I said that we have stopped inviting Mother Nature to the party? We have replaced Mother Nature with ticking clocks and C-sections. Mother Nature has her own way of doing things, particularly when it comes to whelping. She takes her time and she allows mom to recoup her strength, energy and supplies of oxytocin and parathyroid hormone as needed. This recouping and resupplying process sometimes necessitates rest periods. The key is in watching your mom. Is she napping and allowing her babies to nurse? Is she occasionally cleaning their little bottoms and stimulating them? Is the answer is yes to these questions, why in the world would your first assumption be that there is a problem that necessitates major abdominal surgery? Gee. Mom is napping and the babies are fine. Let's cut her! The clock says so.

## Back when grandma was a kid…

I am luckier than most because a couple of dog breeders raised me. I sometimes meet other people at my seminars who were raised by dog breeders. I always ask them to identify themselves by raised hands. Then I ask them how many C-sections their dog breeder parents ever had to do. The answer? Far better than 99% of the time, the answer is zero—never, nada, not at all, zip. My parents bred Chihuahuas and Cocker Spaniels until I was in my late teens and they never had a C-section on a bitch. They never lost a bitch in a whelp either and their puppy losses were no more than average. Some of our bitches whelped quickly, and some whelped slowly, but they all free whelped and no one ever gave a thought to a C-section. It was not unusual for us to all go to bed thinking that all of the puppies had arrived only to wake up the next morning to find another puppy or two happily nursing with the other puppies. It is not that uncommon for a bitch to deliver her litter and then 24, 28 and even 30 hours later deliver another puppy or two. It happens. Does it happen often? No. It does not happen often, but it surely does happen every day throughout the world. So, how do we know when a bitch is in trouble and when she is not? How do we know when a puppy is in trouble and when he is not? Are we willing to cut our precious bitch before we even think there is a problem? Are we willing to put our moms at risk to save our puppies? Is there ever a need for a C-section? Yes, but not nearly at the rate they are being performed.

## How do you know if a bitch is in trouble?

First, let us establish that there is a big difference between when a bitch is in trouble and a puppy is in trouble. The two are not interchangeable. When a bitch is in trouble she will let you know it in several ways—some very subtle and some not subtle at all. A puppy in trouble is completely different. There is almost no way for you to know if a puppy is in trouble and not even the decreasing heart rates that so many vets apparently use as their indicator of problems is reliable. After all, head compression and compression of the cord will both cause fetal heart rate decelerations. Decelerations of heart rate are not a reliable indicator of problems with a puppy anymore than they are a reliable indication of problems with a human baby. This is just one more misconception that has come about because fetal monitors are being used by people who have never worked at the bedside of human moms for whom those machines were designed.

A bitch in trouble will be restless. She will seek eye contact with you to communicate her distress. She will probably be pacing and agitated. She may pace a while and then stop and push for a few seconds. She will not settle and she will ignore her puppies if some have been already whelped. Green discharge is not a sign of trouble. How can it be when canine placentas have so much green coloring that there is an actual name for it: "utero verdin?" Unfortunately, because of that silly myth about not waiting more than two to three hours between puppies before sectioning the bitch, an awful lot of bitches are sectioned when they are not in trouble at all. These bitches are napping with their babies, feeding them, cleaning their little bottoms and resting.

Why is the concept of whelping so entrenched with misunderstandings? I don't really know. I suspect it is partly because our tendencies are to confuse human situations with dog situations. For instance, the green discharge issue: In a human delivery, green amniotic fluid is a sign of fetal distress to one extent or another. It shows us that at some time in the gestational or birth process, the fetus has lost consciousness and consequently his rectal sphincter muscle relaxed and allowed bowel contents to leave his body and enter into the amniotic fluid that surrounds him. This can mean that this baby is brain damaged. We do not have green tissue on our placentas. Green is an unnatural color during the normal birth situation of a human and is always a bad sign. Green amniotic fluid or discharge does not mean the same thing in the bitch. Canine placentas have a lot of green tissue in them. The part that faces the puppy is a deep, murky green. As the puppy readies for delivery by dislodging from the placenta, and as the placenta deteriorates as a part of the natural birth process, green discharge or green tinged amniotic fluid is common, normal, natural and not a sign of anything but whelping.

There is no doubt that puppies are often in distress and end up dead. If we routinely gave birth to multiples our losses would also increase. Some 30% of all puppies born die during or shortly after birth. The thing that is important to remember is that your priority is your bitch. Make your decision early on. Do not wait until the day of whelping to work it out in your mind whether or not you will put your bitch at risk to save your puppies. No one else can make that decision but you. No one should have to make that decision but you.

Seek the help of your vet if your bitch seems to be in distress. Try to allow her plenty of time between puppies and let her behavior be your guide. Stop watching the clock. You clock is not in labor, nor does it reproduce. Who really cares what it thinks or what it says? Your bitch, on the other hand, will give you loud and clear messages. If she is napping and content with her babies, the message she is giving you is this: I'm fine. I'm caring for my babies. I'm taking a break. I need the break. My body knows what it is doing. Shhh-hhhh. If she is in trouble, she will act like a bitch in trouble, not like a bitch that is tired and needs a rest. Mother Nature has brought free-whelping dogs a long way. Please let her continue on that journey and don't allow our bad medical practices to change our beloved species.

## Stuck puppies

It is a horrifying event when a puppy gets stuck on its way out of the birth canal. When we can feel or see a presenting part and it simply is not budging, we often panic and run off to the vets office for help. If you can see or touch a puppy, that puppy is pretty much committed to a vaginal delivery come hell or high water. Under most circumstances, it isn't good medical practice to pull the puppy backward from the birth canal back into the uterus and through the incision. It introduces a tremendous amount of bacteria into the uterus. For the most part, a stuck puppy will need to be delivered vaginally whether you deliver the puppy or the vet does it. Frequently the first puppy down the chute is the one who encounters trouble because the puppies in the lower portion of the horn grow the largest and are therefore the most likely to be stuck.

Think back to when you had a puppy get stuck. These puppies are usually born out of their sack. The component that is missing most of the time with a stuck puppy is the lubrication of the amniotic sac and fluid. You can replace the lubrication by filling a 20 cc syringe with a liquid lubricant and attaching a feeding tube. You can use KY Jelly too, but it needs warming a bit in order to flow through the syringe. Attach a clear silicone feeding tube to the syringe and place the syringe well inside the vagina to the point where the puppy's body is. Put all 20 ccs of liquid lubricant into the bitch's vaginal canal. Now, you can begin the following techniques to attempt to remove a stuck puppy from the birth canal:

1.  See if you can palpate the puppy with your hand on the bitch's spine. The puppy is lying directly under the spine of the bitch in the birth canal. Sometimes, particularly on small bitches, you can feel the puppy lying under the spine and by massaging that area toward the vulva,

you can move it along until it gets far enough out that you can see the puppy. You can kind of "milk" it out of the birth canal by pushing it out from the outside of the spine.

2.  On larger bitches, you can glove up, using lubricant on the rectum and on your glove, reach a finger into the rectum, and gently massage the rectal floor. The puppy is directly under the rectal floor and can be palpated with a finger. No matter what your breed is, you will know whether you can fit a finger into the rectum by looking at the size of the feces. If the feces that your dog passes are larger than your finger, then you know your finger will be able to enter the rectum. Be *very gentle* with this technique. The tissue between the rectum and the vagina is very thin and somewhat delicate. Just gently massage the floor of the rectum and soon you will be able to make out the body of the puppy. Gently massage toward the vulva and you may well be able to push the puppy forward to delivery. Be prepared with all the supplies that you need and it will help you not to panic. Be calm, be thoughtful and think things through. Your main goal is to deliver the puppy and to prevent a C-section. Chances are good that if you can get this stuck puppy delivered, the others will come uneventfully.

3.  Using a little lubricant on your fingertip, you can gently "iron" the perineum of the bitch. As soon as you can reach a body part on the pup, you will need to assess the position of the puppy. Remember that puppies need to "dive" out of the birth canal. It does not really matter whether they dive out head first or foot first, they still need to dive out—both feet extended and both feet need to come out at the same time. If they are not headed in the direction of a dive, then you may need to reach in gently and find the little paw that is caught or pull the little nose downwards; whatever gentle action is needed to get the puppy into dive position. Often the simple act of lubricating will urge a puppy forward. Other times you may need to gently reposition a body part. Ironing the perineum will often relax those vaginal tissues just enough to move the puppy forward.

4.  Using your fingertips, you can pull a tiny bit of fur out of the birth canal. Just work to make a little wrinkle of fur all around the puppy body. After you have created a little wrinkle of fur all around the body, just move the body gently side to side and the body will follow that little wrinkle of fur. Repeat this as many times as you need to in order to get the puppy out.

5.  The last technique cannot be used on a bitch that will not back lie for you. Most girls will assume a back lying position, but a few will not. If you can get your bitch to lie on her back, spread her back legs gently apart. This increases the diameter of the pelvic bones. After she has spread her back legs a bit, apply pressure with the palm of your hand to the area immediately above the pubic bone. This pressure will shift the position of the puppy within the bitch just enough to allow you

to pull it forward. When I was a young labor/delivery nurse, we called this method the Wood's maneuver for the Doctor who first described it but now, it is called simply "Supra Pubic Pressure." Breeders who have used this method successfully have described a "popping" sound when a puppy is pulled from the birth canal. Pictured is a stuck puppy kit with its various components.

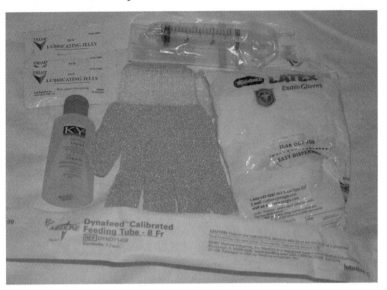

*A stuck puppy kit with its various components.*

# CHAPTER 8
# THE STORY OF SCARLETT

## The Little Clumber That Could

It gives me a great deal of pleasure to include the story of lovely little Scarlet, a little Clumber Spaniel owned by Cindy Brizes. I hope that Cindy's story can inspire you as much as it did me. I did not change a single word of Cindy's story about Scarlett.

It is common for Clumber Spaniel breeders to plan C-sections for whelping puppies. After attending one of Myra Savant-Harris's seminars on breeding and whelping, I became determined to do my best to have a litter of Clumbers naturally whelped.

At the time of the breeding—her first—Scarlett was three years and five months old, so she was heading towards the upper end of her prime breeding years. Scarlett was spending time out in the sun daily, was eating mid-grade kibble, and was not receiving calcium/phosphorous supplements. Based on the results of the Fertile Focus testing and when the estrogen peak occurred, the puppies would be due on December 31, day 63.

With all of the recommended whelping and puppy intensive care items on hand, the expectant human parents awaited the blessed event. At about the time we were getting ready to pop the champagne cork, 11:00 pm on the 31st, Scarlett starting panting and acting uncomfortable. She was very nervous and insisted that I stay in the whelping box with her. The panting continued for several hours. Just before dawn, I decided that the signs were not increasing so I left the box to take a nap. Scarlett went to sleep and slept most of the day on January 1.

At about midnight on January 1, I noticed that it was wet where she had been laying on the dog bed. Could this be the water breaking? About 30 minutes later, she was back in the whelping box, panting and thrashing about, very uncomfortable. At 12:30 am on January 2, she pushed out a water sac about the size of a golf ball. I began to get nervous and started sending e-mails to Myra—thank goodness she is on the other coast and was still checking messages! She reminded me to be patient and stop watching the clock. I had other friends that were recommending that I head for the emergency vet and a C-section, but Myra convinced me to stay calm and be patient.

At 2:45 am, Scarlett was showing signs of contractions and pushing. After about 45 minutes of this, I was getting worried and fired off another e-mail. Myra recommended giving Scarlett Calsorb, and then do my best to check for a stuck puppy. I gave Scarlett the Calsorb and then gloved up to check for a puppy. I had no idea what I was supposed to actually be feeling for. I started the exam and could feel something, but what? The cervix, another water sac, what? Then it hit me, it was the mouth of a puppy! The puppy was in the birth canal. Stuck? Now I started to panic, dug out my whelping book by Myra and re-read the section on un-sticking puppies. I was in the process of getting the KY jelly and a feeding tube ready for gooping up the puppy, as well as waking up my husband for assistance, when Scarlett started to push out the puppy. It was a large puppy and I helped by gently pulling on the puppy while going around the vulva pushing the skin back. At 3:45 am, the first puppy arrived. How exciting to get the first puppy out naturally! I helped Scarlett to open the sac, clean the puppy and cut the umbilical cord.

After that, Scarlett had one puppy about every hour. She totally took over cleaning and cord duties. By late morning, Scarlett had naturally whelped eight puppies! The news of the natural whelping spread through the Clumber Spaniel community, hopefully inspiring others to be patient, let nature do the work, and whelp naturally if at all possible.

At over three weeks of age, all eight puppies are doing well and growing strong. We look forward to another litter (naturally) with Scarlett next year.

*Scarlett and her puppies.*

# Chapter 9
# Milk Production

## Get it In, Get it Out and Kiss it Goodbye

You would think that anything as common as breast milk would be easy to produce and easy to manage, but in truth it is not easy for some of our girls. Some bitches simply do not produce milk and some produce limited quantities—but not enough to feed their puppies. Some bitches are filled with milk, but it is impossible to remove any of it when necessary, and some bitches stay filled with milk for several days after the puppies are weaned. While it is usually an automatic process, it can also present some puzzling situations. Breeders feel more empowered when they are well educated and well prepared to solve a milk-production problem well before they encounter it.

*A litter of healthy puppies nursing.*

I breast-fed some of my children and it was actually an easy process. Because it was easy for me and easy for my babies, I assumed it was an easy process for all moms. That attitude left me poorly prepared for the situations I met a few years later while working in labor and delivery. I am grateful for the education that the lactation specialists and the moms and babies who struggled shared with me.

When I started breeding dogs, I was at least aware of the problems that I had seen as a labor/delivery nurse, but initially I did not have any easy solutions for bitches with milk-production issues. It took a lot of time, a lot of reading and discussions with a number of other experienced breeders who shared their experiences before I finally began to comprehend the process of milk-production, milk removal from the breast, and how to dry out a bitch who has produced milk that is no longer needed.

## Why won't my bitch produce milk?

There are several reasons why a bitch does not produce any milk, or can't produce enough milk, but the majority of us are only going to have to deal with a few of them. Often a girl will have milk, but just not enough of it to feed her litter. Sometimes these litters are larger than usual for the breed. Some girls will eventually produce milk, but because of a C-section done a few days too early or due to the whelping of a premature litter, the milk is just not there in time. Sometimes a girl will have become somewhat dehydrated during the whelping and delivery and will need assistance with both hydration and milk production.

First on your agenda should be making sure your bitch is drinking enough water. Of course, eating is part of the picture as well, but even a recently whelped mom can miss a few meals without it affecting her or her puppies. None of the girls can be dehydrated for long, however, before it impacts the health status of both mom and babies. If your bitch seems reluctant to drink sufficient quantities of water, try flavoring it with a nice dollop of goats milk or another milk product. That often entices them to drink. You can try putting some low sodium chicken broth in the water too.

A milk-producing bitch requires significantly more water per day than a non milk-producing bitch. Unfortunately, there doesn't seem to be any research out there on how much water is required to produce milk in the canine. But, for example, a cow needs to drink approximately 20 gallons of water per day in order to produce approximately 7 gallons of milk, while maintaining her own body weight. This figure reflects the cow's water requirements at an ambient temperature of 70 degrees or so. As the temperature goes up, the cow needs more water in order to produce this same amount of milk. From this statistic, we can clearly see that a lactating bitch need to have access to more water while lactating than at any other time in her life.

## Fenugreek

After you have made sure that she is consuming adequate amounts of water, you can begin the use of a homeopathic food supplement to assist her to bring in the milk in the quantity needed by her puppies. Fenugreek is what the La Leche League recommends for nursing human moms and it works on bitches as well. Do not use Fenugreek prior to whelping.

Women have been using Fenugreek as a supplement to aid in milk production since at least 2000 years BC. The fenugreek plant produces a seed used in various forms for thousands of years to make teas or were crushed and consumed when women needed to increase their milk production. Modern Fenugreek comes in teas, crushed and powdered in clear capsules. The ground seeds are light and powdery with almost no taste. The taste is sort of "plantie," but not objectionable. The odor of the ground fenugreek seed is quite distinctive and rather pleasant. It smells like maple syrup, a fact that is important for the breeder to note.

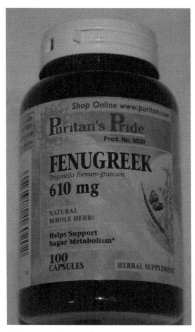

*Fenugreek supplement*

The capsule dose that I have seen most often is 610 mg. The La Leche League's web site, www.lalecheleague.com, has interesting articles about Fenugreek and its role in milk production. Because Fenugreek is widely available in health food stores (and on my web site: www.myrasavantharris.com) and is considered to be a safe and effective food supplement, it is the first thing that I would recommend to any breeder who is having a problem with milk production in a bitch. If the Fenugreek fails, then I would seek the recommendation of your vet who might prescribe Reglan, a medication used widely in humans to increase the peristalsis of the intestine. It works quite well to increase milk production in both humans and dogs. Reglan can cause severe diarrhea in dogs, and for that reason I would consider it as a secondary medication versus a primary solution to the problem.

## How much Fenugreek do I give?

When food supplements designed for people are given to dogs, the dosing is always somewhat problematic because there is so little information and documentation. There are not any studies on the amount of Fenugeek to give a bitch but, because it is a food supplement and considered to be quite safe, there is a fair amount of leeway on the amounts we can safely administer. *Your goal is to give enough Fenugreek to cause the breath and milk of the bitch to smell like maple syrup.* Sometimes the odor is strong enough that when you walk into the room you can smell maple syrup. For very small dogs like Chihuahuas, Yorkies, Maltese, start with a single 610 mg capsule, opened and sprinkled on a tasty food. Give it with breakfast and again with lunch. Before each dose, check her breath and general odor. If she does not have a maple syrup fragrance, then add a bit more to her next meal. Usually one to two capsules given morning, noon and night will bring in milk on a toy dog. For a medium sized dog, you may have to administer three capsules morning, lunch and dinner and for a very large dog, you may have to administer as many as five of the capsules. You can either give the capsules whole (hidden in food works well) or opened and sprinkled on food. Two to three hours after each dose, check for the odor of maple syrup. When the bitch's breath has a strong smell of maple syrup, the dose is right. There are usually no side effects, but occasionally the fenugreek will cause a bitch to vomit. Once milk production is well established, there is no need to continue giving the Fenugreek. If milk production appears to decrease, you can simply return to the dose you were giving her when her milk came in.

### "Mother's Pudding"

Many breeders have given "Mother's Pudding" to their bitches to assist in milk production with success. It is certainly worth the small amount of time necessary to prepare it and definitely falls into the category of: can't hurt, might help. Here is the recipe for Mother's Pudding:

- One small package of vanilla pudding (the kind you use for cooking).
- ½ cup sugar.
- 4 cups of milk.
- 4 egg yolks.

Cook until it comes to a boil and then remove from stove to cool. Feed when cool. Because there is sugar in this recipe, it can cause diarrhea, so if your bitch is sensitive to sugary foods, consider using a sugar free pudding.

## When do I need to remove milk from the breast?

There are just a few situations in which a breeder would need to remove milk from the breast of the bitch. However, even those few situations can be frustrating and worrisome if you do not have any information about the process. One situation would be when a bitch loses an entire litter. It's likely her milk production may be overwhelming for her. Breasts that are full of milk can be very uncomfortable for the girls. If your bitch produces milk following the death of her litter, make every attempt to remove some of the colostrum from each breast and freeze it for use on future litters. It will stay good in the normal household freezer for at least six months and longer at zero degrees. It contains all of the immunities that moms give to their puppies and can be used by any puppies, any breed. It can safely be tube fed or bottle fed to any baby who failed to get colostrum from its own mom.

If a mom develops mastitis in one or more breasts, it would be advisable to remove milk from the affected breasts as recommended by your vet before allowing the litter to nurse from the remaining nipples. If a mom becomes engorged for any reason, the removal of a small amount of milk will give her relief until the babies begin to remove the excess. Sometimes premature puppies lack a suck reflex until they catch up with their gestational age and being able to remove milk and/or colostrum from mom's breast will be very useful to you. You can also feed these puppies a formula.

## How do I get milk out of the breast?

Expressing milk from the breast is reasonably easy with some bitches. It is next to impossible with others, but it is very time consuming even under the best of circumstances. If you are unable to express milk from the breast, the use of a little canine breast pump can often do the trick.

The breast will need to be completely fur free. Removal of the hair is essential prior to using the breast pump. Warm, wet washcloths applied directly to the breasts help to get milk ready to flow when you use the breast pump. These little breast pumps are easy to make and the syringes are easy to find. They do not look like much in their completed form, but they work well. You can use a three cc syringe for very small girls and on up to a 30 cc syringe for very large girls. The syringe used to make the breast pump is nothing more than a regular medical syringe. Syringes break down into the "barrel" and the "plunger." Take the syringe apart and, using a small saw, remove the top portion of the barrel. Remove about the top ¼ to ½ inch of the barrel. Then smooth those edges down with a piece of fine grade sandpaper. After you have smoothed down the edges, replace the plunger into the cut off and sanded end. Place the flanged end of the barrel against the bitch's bare breast and pull the plunger back and forth in a pumping action to effect a suction pump that facilitates removal of the milk. Practice on your arm a couple of times to get the feeling for use of the breast pump. You can make these pumps in very little time and with little expense except for the saw blades. The saw blades do not last very long because the plastic in the syringes melts with the friction of the saw so the blades are the real expense in the canine breast pumps.

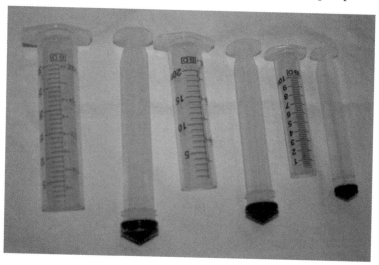

*Medical syringes modified for breast milk removal.*

## How do I dry up my bitch?

If you need to help your bitch with the drying process, there are some things that you can do to help her. It is not a good idea to restrict her water intake because it is simply too difficult to judge the hydration needs of each bitch. My recommended method is a homeopathic one and can help bitches to stop milk production. Give the bitch plain old rubbed sage, which can you can purchase in just about any grocery store and is located in the spice aisle. (It is especially easy to find during the Thanksgiving and Christmas holidays because it is the same sage as is used in recipes to stuff turkeys for holiday dinners.) Because it is a homeopathic method and because bitches come in every size from as small as four pounds up to large bitches of 220 pounds or so, dosing is really a matter of educated guess work and good luck. Sage, however, can be consumed in large quantities without ill effects. (Ask any of us an hour after finishing Thanksgiving dinner. The turkey was stuffed. We were stuffed and all of us except the turkey lived to tell the tale.)

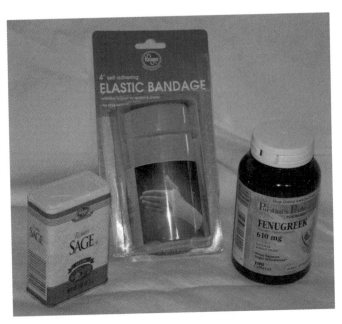

*Sage, bandage and Fenugreek.*

Start with giving a half-teaspoon of sage sprinkled over tasty food for very small dogs and go up to as much as two full tablespoons sprinkled over food for large dogs. Give this in the morning, at lunch and at dinner. As soon as you have started giving the sage over the food, also begin wrapping the mid-section of the bitch with an elastic bandage. Ace elastic bandages can be found in drug stores and most grocery stores. Choose the size that is best for your particular breed. The most common sizes vary from two inches to six inches. Wrap the mid-section, being careful to cover all of the breast tissue. If necessary, use two wraps. *Do not use the little clips that come with the elastic bandages.* They can become dislodged and end up being swallowed by the dog. Use diaper pens or very large safety pins and be sure that they are pinned to the back portion of the dog. The girls can reach their tummies. Be sure that you can place a finger between the bitch and the wrap, but you definitely need to make sure that the bandage does compress the breast tissue. If the breasts are compressed with the elastic bandage, there is no room for the milk and the bitch will dry up quickly.

## Mastitis

If your bitch develops mastitis, there are things you can do to speed up the healing process. Most bitches with mastitis will require an antibiotic prescribed by your vet in order to help their bodies fight infection in their breasts. Give the antibiotic as directed by your vet until every dose has been given. It is completely safe to give sage to a bitch who is taking an antibiotic if you need to dry up her breasts. Infected breasts are *always* helped by the application of wet, warm washcloths or hand towels held directly on the affected breasts. Hold the warm packs on to the breast tissue for at least fifteen minutes at a time. Thirty-minute sessions are better. The warm packs need to be applied at least three times a day and four times daily is better. If you can handle the warm packs with your *bare hands,* the temperature of the water will not be too hot for your bitch. This is how you will always know the warm packs are safe for your bitch. I know it is a lot of work and very time consuming, but the healing time is faster when warm packs are used.

The application of moist heat not only gives pain relief and comfort to your bitch, but warm packs also aid in ridding the body of infection. As the infected tissue warms from the application of the warm pack, the vascular system expands and this facilitates faster and more efficient drainage from the area. Along with an antibiotic, a "drawing poultice" is also more helpful than you might think. After hot packing the affected breast tissue, warm cabbage leaves slightly by rolling them in your hands. Then, place the cabbage leaves directly on to the infected breast tissue and hold them in place with the elastic bandages. The cabbage leaves help to "draw" the infected fluids out of the breast tissues.

I didn't have much faith in the use of cabbage leaves until I met a young vet at one of my seminars. She told me about her own use of cabbage leaves held in place by her bra after she was diagnosed with mastitis and after hearing her story, I knew that it was safe to recommend their use to you. They cabbage leaves do, indeed, work. She did me a huge service by sharing her story with me. I believe in using methods that are inexpensive, easy to use and harmless right along with the medications and other treatments that are recommended by our vets. These techniques are easy to perform and the things you need are readily available. From everything that breeders have told me, I know that they will help your bitch. They fall into the category of: can't hurt, might help, but they lean heavily toward the helpful category.

## Milk substitutes

If nothing you have done helps to increase the milk supply of your bitch, you will have to resort to milk substitutes. It is possible to raise a puppy without breast milk. If your puppies did not receive colostrum from your bitch, then you will need to arrange to use a substitute for the colostrum and do it within the first three days of life. You can use either colostrum taken from another bitch within 24 hours of her own whelping day. You can also use fresh frozen plasma (FFP) either tube fed to the puppies within 24 hours of their birth or administered subcutaneously, or you can take mom and babies to your vet where he can draw mom's blood, spin it down to a clear serum and inject the clear serum into the puppies. This will help to ensure that your puppies get the immunities from their mom that are needed until they are old enough for vaccinations.

There are canned milk substitutes for puppies. Formulas such as Esbilac and Just Born are easily obtained from pet catalogues and in pet stores. They have made every attempt to duplicate the nutrition and calories found naturally in breast milk. They are a useful substitute, but my homemade formula, discussed on page 69, is a better one.

## Why do hand-raised puppies grow so slowly?

Whenever I have raised puppies by hand, I noticed that their growth rates are very erratic and slow. Days after birth, they still have that newborn puppy look. While their littermates are filling out and becoming plumper by the day, my hand-raised puppies are still thin. Growth is slow and seems to occur in little spurts. This has puzzled and frustrated me because I am dutiful in tube feeding the puppy around the clock. Of course, these hand-raised puppies usually have some other problem or I would not be hand raising them to begin with, but that does not seem to be a good excuse for the puppy not gaining weight.

I began to watch the breast feeding process very carefully to see which part I was missing on hand raised puppies. It became clear to me rather quickly that newborns nurse for hours every day. Their abdomens stay rounded and full all day and all night—full, full, full, full. My little hand raised puppies were being fed every two to four hours depending on the individual puppy, but their little tummies didn't stay rounded and full all day and all night. Instead, their abdomens appeared to empty between feedings and round out when I tube fed them—empty, full, empty, full, empty, full—24 hours a day. It became obvious to me that puppies nurse vigorously when first on the nipple but, as their tummies fill, they slow down and settle into sort of a lazy little suck pattern. They sleep with their mouths on the nipple and ever so often, they give a lazy little suck. The stomach of a newborn puppy is full almost all the time. It never completely empties. Every time a drop of milk goes from the stomach into the intestine, the puppy gives a lazy little suck and replaces that drop. Obviously, they take in many calories nursing in that manner.

## Best choice? A homemade puppy formula

So how can we keep the growth rate of hand-raised puppies on a comparable level with breast-fed puppies? We can't leave a feeding tube in place at all times as we do in intensive care units. How do we make sure the puppy gets the same amount of calories per day that a breast-fed puppy gets? The answer: Keep the caloric intake of the puppy on a par with his breast fed littermates by increasing the number of calories per cc in our puppy formula.

Here is a puppy formula that increases the calories per cc from the three to four calories per cc found in breast milk and commercially prepared formula. It contains ten to twelve calories per cc, contains live culture yogurt to prevent diarrhea, Karo syrup to prevent constipation, and a meat product with important amino acids that will avoid the formation of juvenile cataracts caused by nutritional deficits. In addition, puppies like it and it can be frozen and used as needed. It has all the vitamins that a growing baby needs and the things needed to prepare it are easily available. Baby vitamins can be located in the grocery store on the baby supply aisle or in almost any drug store. Canned evaporated goat's milk can be found in the same location as canned evaporated cow's milk in the grocery store—usually the baking aisle. This formula has been well vetted and approved by a number of veterinarians and many breeders. You will notice a weight gain about 48 hours after the first feeding, but once he starts growing, he will grow like a little weed. It is more time consuming than opening a can of commercially prepared formula, but it will really pay off when you see a significant weight gain on the puppy.

This formula is safe for any age from the tiniest premature baby to the most elderly dog. It can remain in the freezer for up to six months. I have never met a dog who does not love it or a puppy who didn't gain weight quickly while eating it. Because so many breeders have reported that the administration of "liver water" appears to strengthen fading puppies, I am including it in the formula, but I am also including a quick substitute for liver water if you are "liver phobic." Liver water is made by boiling a nice piece of beef or calves liver in a couple of cups of water until the liver is well cooked and the water has reduced to about one cup. Strain the liver water and freeze whatever you don't use for use next time you prepare this formula. Here is the recipe:

- 1/3 cup of strong homemade beef broth (best made with liver).

- 1 can evaporated goat's milk (can substitute evaporated cow's milk). *Do not dilute!*

- 1 cup of whole fat live culture yogurt (the higher the fat content the better).

- 2 raw egg yolks.

- 1 tablespoon of mayonnaise or canola oil.

- 1 teaspoon of Karo syrup or corn syrup (any color).

- 1 teaspoon of baby vitamins.

Place all ingredients into a blender and blend until completely mixed. Pour formula into ice cube trays and freeze. When the cubes are frozen, take them out of the ice cube tray and place into a heavy weight plastic bag. At each feeding, take enough cubes to make a feeding, place them into a plastic bag (snack sized Ziplocs work best) and warm to a temperature of approximately 95 to 96 degrees, luke warm. If you are tube feeding, you can connect the tube to the syringe and use the end of the tube to remove the formula from the snack bag. If you are bottle-feeding, just pour the warmed formula into the bottle. This puppy formula has ten to twelve calories per cc and will put weight on your puppies. You will not have diarrhea or constipation with this formula. If you can put the necessary time into it, you will be very, very happy with the outcomes.

## How do I feed a newborn?

First choice: Breast-feeding from mom, so use all of your skills to accomplish this before you resort to other choices. Do whatever it takes to bring milk in on mom and do the best you can to help baby to latch on to the nipple. This may represent quite a lot of time and work at first, but it will pay off big time once baby can nurse on his own.

Second choice: Bottle feeding the baby is your next best choice simply because it will preserve the puppy's suck reflex. The baby is also the best guide as to how much food he needs at any feeding and he can best manage this with a bottle. Bottle fed babies often eat more formula per feeding and eat fewer times a day than tubed babies. Be sure to burp a bottle fed puppy and make sure you actually hear the little burp.

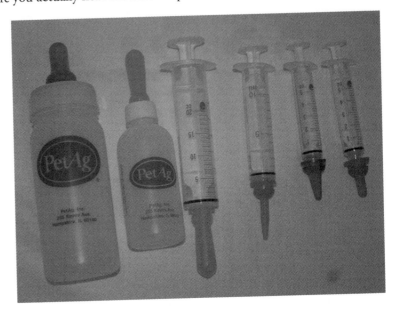

*Some of the available options for bottle feeding.*

Third choice: Tube feeding is your third choice, but often ends up our only choice. If baby does not have a strong suck reflex at birth or if he has a tiny little cleft in his palate, he may not be able to suck and tube feeding becomes a lifesaver. Tube feeding is covered at length in my *Puppy Intensive Care* book, including a video of me tubing a newborn puppy. If you are nervous, watch it over and over until you feel confident.

*Feeding a puppy with an eyedropper is simply not an option.* Puppies, like all babies have an instinct to suck. Sucking involves wrapping the tongue around the nipple, pulling the nipple into the back of the mouth held in place between the tongue and the palate. Puppies swallow from the back of their throats, not from the front of their mouths. Puppies do not have the skills necessary to use their tongues to push formula to the back of the throat for swallowing. If thin liquids are placed in the front of their mouths with syringes or eyedroppers, the liquid will end up in the lungs as often as in the stomach. This will lead to aspiration pneumonia and your puppy will die. Stick to one of the three viable choices for feeding a newborn and your puppy will appreciate it.

# CHAPTER 10
# GLUCOSE AND DEHYDRATION

## Low Blood Sugar and Dehydration
## Always Go Hand in Hand

Glucose is stored in the liver and released into the blood stream as needed. The mechanism to store glucose, sense the need for it, and release it into the blood stream is pretty complex. It should not really be too surprising to know that premature babies, very small puppies and weakened puppies may not be able to keep up with the blood glucose needs of their bodies. (Blood glucose and blood sugar are interchangeable and mean the same thing.) Every dog breeder needs to have a good glucose source for use on puppies at their fingertips at all times. Your glucose source should be easily obtained, inexpensive and clean to use. If a puppy appears to be suffering from low blood sugar, you can bet the farm that he is dehydrated as well. The two—low blood glucose and dehydration are like a set of evil twins when it comes to puppies. If you see one, you can be certain the other is lurking nearby. You need to be able to "fix" them both immediately.

## Decorator frosting—who knew?

This is just one more example of a wonderful piece of information that I was given by another dog breeder. This breeder in South Carolina happened to be a diabetic and carried with him a small container of the type of decorator frosting used on cakes that comes in those little boxes. His diabetic doctor had recommended that he carry a little tube of frosting in his pocket to use at times when he felt his own blood sugar was getting low. These little tubes of frosting are glucose with harmless food coloring added. The invaluable tip that

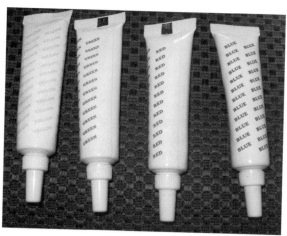

*Tubes of frosting can help supply a puppy with glucose.*

he shared at one of my seminars was that the decorator frosting could also be used to supply glucose your puppies when they display signs of low blood sugar.

It is not necessary to perform a blood test to see if your puppy is low on blood sugar. If the puppy is significantly low on blood sugar, you do not have time to get to the vet and have the test processed. Low blood sugar begins to kill brain cells if left unattended. High blood sugar kills too, but it takes its slow easy time about it and kills off a system or an organ one at a time. Low blood sugar can kill a puppy right now! The brains of mammals metabolize only glucose. Glucose is the only food that the brain actually utilizes. Low blood sugar levels can starve the brain to death—quite literally. Low blood sugar will certainly make your puppy look almost dead. If you combine low blood sugar with dehydration the puppy will be limp, vital signs will have slowed, and the puppy will appear to be almost lifeless.

So, my recommendation is that if the puppy appears to be weak, fading or otherwise impaired in any way, first give a little dose of glucose by wiping the frosting on the puppy's tongue. It is that simple. Just wipe a little of the frosting from the tube on the puppy's tongue and wait fifteen minutes. If the puppy is suffering from low blood glucose levels, that little dab of frosting on his tongue will help him within five minutes. At the first sign that his status is improving, put another little dab of frosting on his tongue. Once you have seen glucose at work and have seen how quickly it can restore a puppy that looks as if he is one or two thready little heart beats from death, you will never want to be without it. A puppy in need of glucose can appear to be anything from just sleepy to comatose. Low blood sugar can cause seizure activity. Administer a little dab of frosting on the tongue every three to four hours on premature puppies, puppies who are very small for gestational age (the real term for what we call "runt"), fading puppies or puppies who appear to have a weakened status as would be evidenced by poor or weak suck reflex.

## Frosting is magic in so many ways
There is another purpose for using the colored frosting tubes. The coloring provides you with an amazingly accurate and useful little assessment tool. (All nurses are very big on "assessment tools.") If a puppy appears to be ill, choose a color from your box of frostings. Administer it by just wiping a small amount on the puppy's tongue. It is hard to be exact about the amount you wipe on the tongue, but think of it in very general terms—for a toy, wipe an amount about the size of a match head. For a larger puppy, use a dab about as large as a pea. Repeat this dose as soon as the puppy begins to respond to it by becoming more active and lively looking. Keep a little chart and mark the time of the administration of the first dose of glucose. Keep this puppy separated from the other puppies. You would want to do this anyhow until the puppy looks and acts normal. Note the time of his next bowel movement. Note its color. If the puppy has blue poop in half an hour to an hour of the time you first put blue frosting on its tongue, you will know immediately that the puppy has diarrhea.

If the puppy has diarrhea you can begin the process of sorting out all the reasons why he would be dehydrated. Diarrhea can be a killer if it goes undetected because it leaches out the electrolytes that are found in the stomach acids and carries away fluids leading to dehydration. It does not take long for a small puppy to develop a serious electrolyte imbalance coupled with dehydration. Your very first step is to stop feeding the puppy until his bowel movements look somewhat normal. Your second step is to treat the diarrhea. Your vet may have medications that work well, but for this scenario we are returning to the favorite time for dog and puppy emergencies: Friday night on a holiday weekend in the middle of a blizzard, earthquake, hurricane, take your pick. You are alone and cannot reach the vet's clinic. If your vet will agree to it, you can ask him in advance for a small supply of a good medication for diarrhea and keep it in your "war chest."

Preparation is everything when breeding dogs and this is just one more example of how your little "war chest" filled with supplies will assist you in saving your puppy. "The Pink Stuff" is one very good remedy for diarrhea and so is Kaopectate. Many breeders have written to me to tell me that Kaopectate contains aspirin and indeed, it does. Aspirin is safe if given in small amounts and is an excellent anti-inflammatory for the bowel wall. When diarrhea is present, the walls of the intestines become inflamed. The more inflamed those tissues become the more severe the diarrhea is. Stopping the inflammation is key to "fixing" diarrhea and there are many medications and supplements that are very useful for soothing the intestinal tract. Ask your vet for advice.

*The Pink Stuff: A handy remedy for diarrhea.*

You can tube feed a liquid medication if the puppy is still young enough to tube feed. If the puppy is strong enough to bottle feed, add a small amount of formula and administer it by bottle. Kaopectate can also be tube fed. With its combination of aspirin to soothe and clay to absorb, Kaopectate can be an asset to all dog breeders. After you have begun to treat the diarrhea, keep accurate records of how often the puppy poops. You can track the time it takes things to get from the stomach to the rectum by the colors of the frosting. Change the color of the frosting after the bowel movements slow and become more solid. Once you are able to reach your vet, these records will be very useful to her.

Let me set up a little scenario that has been experienced by many dog breeders. Of course, the last thing you did before you went to bed was to check your puppies and everybody looked fine. First thing in the morning, you discover a puppy down. He is not nursing, he is off by himself and not in the usual puppy heap. His eyes are dull and he appears to be very weak. His muscle tone is slack. He may have suffered an injury of some sort during the night, but the most likely thing to have happened is that he has become dehydrated and his blood sugar is low. During the night, bigger or stronger puppies might have bumped him off the nipple. If he was not able to nurse during the night, he automatically would have become dehydrated. If he does not get a steady diet of breast milk, with its high glucose level, he will automatically become dehydrated. If he also has diarrhea, he will be dehydrated with low blood sugar and possibly low on electrolytes as well.

This puppy looks like he is near death; you can be almost certain that he is dehydrated and has low blood sugar. You can fix this, but you absolutely need to be prepared before the emergency occurs. By the time you have chased down the supplies you need, your puppy may have stepped over the threshold between life and death. You did not prepare for the emergency that is staring you in the face. Make a list now of things you may need and start gathering things that you will need in emergencies well before the date of whelping. It will give you more confidence if you know you have prepared yourself for emergencies and it will save lives.

## Dehydration

It is easy for puppies to become dehydrated. They latch on to a nipple for many hours a day. If they miss a couple of meals, their fluid levels get low and they become dehydrated. Because breast milk has glucose in it, they will also get hypoglycemic if they get dehydrated. If a puppy has poor muscle tone and appears to be ill, it is important to refrain from putting food in his stomach until he has responded to care. Once a puppy can position himself for comfort, has a blink reflex, and feels warm to the touch, you can begin feeding him by mouth. (Whether his eyes are open or not, he will exhibit a blink reflex if you lightly tap the skin around his eyes.) Until that time, you should use warmed IV fluids to hydrate him subcutaneously; under his skin. You can administer a little bit of glucose on his tongue and you can tube feed him medications for diarrhea if he has very loose stools, but you should not put large quantities of food in his stomach until he has exhibited signs that he is improving. Whether you feed him or administer fluids subcutaneously, you need to use the same amount of fluid: One cc per ounce of body weight. Put food in his stomach every three to four hours, or more often if he cries as if he is hungry. Use a syringe and needle to place fluid under his skin at the same rate; one cc per ounce of body weight every three to four hours. It is easy to know if you need to place more fluid. If the bubble of fluid from the previous subcutaneous administration is still present and can be palpated with your finger, you should not administer more. If it disappears within ten minutes or so, you should replace it because fast absorption is a sign of severe dehydration.

Please review the information from this chapter and the information included in my first book, *Puppy Intensive Care.*

## Summary

1. Puppies need warmth. Keep them at about 95 degrees until they reach three weeks of age.

2. Puppies need glucose. If the puppy appears to be weak, fading or sick, use frosting as a quick, easily obtainable source of glucose. Wipe a little on the tongue.

3. Discuss diarrhea treatments with your vet and be prepared to treat diarrhea at its first sign.

4. Gasping puppies will benefit from having oxygen on hand.

5. Puppies need fluids at the rate of one cc per ounce of body weight every three to four hours.

6. Do not feed a chilled or extremely weak puppy. He will bloat.

7. Most fading puppies are dehydrated and hypoglycemic.

8. Breast-feeding is best for the puppy. Second best is bottle-feeding because it preserves the suck reflex. You'll be surprised at the amount of food that a bottle feeding puppy will ingest. If a puppy is unable to suck, tube feeding is a wonderful substitute. (Covered in *Puppy Intensive Care*.)

9. The puppy can only stay on clear fluids for 24 hours or so. After that, he needs a feeding that contains protein. The puppy formula in this chapter is the best thing to use.

10. Feeding a sick puppy can easily lead to his death if his body is not ready for feedings by mouth. If the peristalsis in his gut has not returned to full function, he will bloat and this will often lead to a cascade of symptoms leading to death. Here are the three signs that you can watch for before resuming feedings by mouth:

    - He must be able to reposition himself for comfort. He must be able to move his little body parts in order to feel more comfortable.

    - He must feel warm to the touch.

    - He must have a "blink" reflex. Even puppies whose eyes are still sealed can demonstrate a blink reflex if you lightly tap around his eyes. You'll see the skin there "blink." Blink reflexes are an important sign for him to exhibit before you start feeding him by mouth.

# CHAPTER 11
# PUPPY RESUSCITATION

## Delees, Accordions, Needles and Midgets

Sometimes puppies come to us looking like they are dead and just waiting for us to dispose of the bodies. Some of these puppies can be resuscitated and brought back from the brink of death with good techniques, rapid reaction times and appropriate supplies. I hope that after you have read this chapter, all of you will stop swinging and shaking down puppies and switch over to better techniques that are more likely to save them and less likely to hurt them.

Puppies are born filled with fluid—particularly C-section babies who did not have the benefit of being squeezed a bit as they came down the birth canal. They have been inhaling and swallowing amniotic fluid for weeks. The first step toward resuscitation is to remove that fluid from their airways. There are two great techniques for accomplishing this. Master both of these techniques because you will need to know both methods and be proficient at their uses in order to save puppies.

### Delee suction catheters

The first line of defense against little lungs filled with fluid is the Delee Suction Catheter. (Included on the order sheet at the back of the book.) This little tool will give you the ability to suction fluid from the puppy's mouth, nose and throat. As seen in the photo, the Delee has two tubes that lead out of a clear plastic "trap." The tube with the mouthpiece is for your mouth. The tube with the holes on the end is for the puppy's mouth. With the small mouthpiece in your mouth, and the little tube with the holes in it inside the puppy's mouth, throat and nostrils, you exert suction much as if you were sucking a straw. The little tube can go to wherever there is stuff to suction, including behind the tongue.

Whatever you suction from the mouth of the puppy gets caught in the clear plastic "trap" and nothing will get into your mouth from the suctioning process. The Delee will allow you to suction for several minutes at a time if you need to, as opposed to a bulb syringe, which gives you a nano second of suction. The Delee is usable for an entire litter and can then be taken apart and

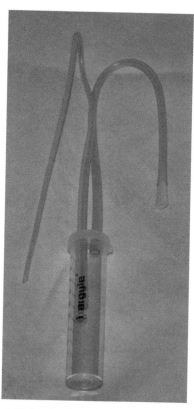

*A Delee Suction Catheter.*

washed with hot, soapy water and allowed to air dry before reassembly. Delee Suction Catheters are usable on puppies of any age for suction purposes. After you have suctioned the puppy's mouth and throat, you are ready to attempt to empty fluid from the lungs. You can do this using the accordion method.

## The accordion method

A vet named Joanna O'Brien designed the "accordion method." She wrote an article for a Chow magazine in the 1970s that described how to use the method that she used to stimulate puppies and empty their lungs of fluid. It is a wonderful technique and is far superior to the horrible shaking down and swinging used by many vets and dog breeders. Using the accordion technique quickly after having used the Delee Suction Catheter to remove mucous and amniotic fluid empties the puppy's lungs of fluids, stimulates the heart and utilizes negative air pressure to pull air into the now empty lungs of the puppy.

Grasp the puppy's back quarters with your dominant hand, hold the puppy's front quarters with you non-dominant hand and hold the puppy head down at about 45 degrees. This lets gravity help to get fluids out. Stretch the little body out gently between the two hands and then push the rear end forward toward the front quarters. Repeat. By gently stretching the puppy's body and then pushing it forward, the lungs will empty and the heart will press between the other internal organs. On the pull back, negative air pressure causes air to flow into the lungs. Practice with a stuffed animal before whelping until you can visualize how the little body is stretched gently back and then pushed gently forward.

*The accordion method, step 1.*

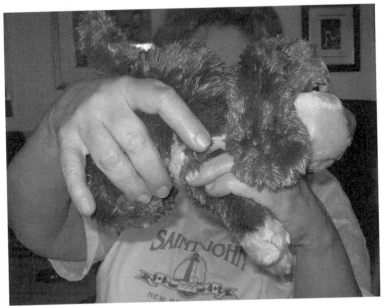

*The accordian method, step 2.*

## Acupuncture

You can also use a little acupuncture technique to stimulate the respiratory system of your puppy. If the puppy is not breathing, this technique is often very successful in stimulating him to take his first breath. Use a sterile, surgical needle. The size I recommend is a 22 gauge, three quarter inch long medical quality needle. Place the needle immediately under the nose leather in the little septum that all puppies have between their noses and the lips. The needle will slide in very easily and will go directly through the lip into the gum. Pull it back slightly out of the gum tissue and then twirl it lightly into the little "dimple" located right under the septum on the gum. This frequently works well and causes the puppy to take a breath. You can substitute acupressure at the same location, but if you do, you will miss an important assessment feature. If the puppy bleeds from the needle hole, it is a very positive sign that this puppy has a circulatory system and is alive in spite of the fact that it may look dead. Continue working on this puppy with all your skills because where there is blood flowing, there is hope.

*The acupuncture method.*

I know that people are often needle phobic. Our memories of injections and blood draws have left many of us wary of needles. However, needle phobic or not, your puppy needs you to do whatever you can do to save him. You cannot possibly hurt him with the needle. Just keep telling yourself: "I can't kill what is already dead, but I may be able to bring this puppy back to life." It will help you to get over your fears of handling needles and get on with the business of saving your puppy. As most of you have learned—breeding dogs is not for the faint of heart.

## Small for gestational age puppies, large for gestational age puppies

After the eggs have been fertilized and have undergone several cell divisions, they begin to drift out of the fallopian tubes and into the uterine horns where they will find an implant spot and begin to grow. This happens somewhere between day 18 and 21. Some of these eggs will find implant sites that are excellent with lots of nutrition available to the puppy. Some of the eggs will land in implant sites that do not enjoy a rich blood supply and the puppy will not grow to normal size. These undersized puppies are called "small for gestational age puppies," or "SGA" puppies. This term tells us much more than the word "runt" tells us.

Bitter experience has taught the veteran dog breeder that the implants sites at the rear of the bitch closest to the vagina are excellent because puppies implanted at the rear end of the uterine horns often grow so large that they get stuck in the birth canal and often die during the birth process. These big babies are called "large for gestational age puppies," or "LGA" puppies and are often first out.

*SGA, average size and LGA puppies from the same litter.*

LGA puppies frequently create delivery issues because they get stuck on the way out and present something of a log jam for remaining littermates, but once they arrive, they are usually just fine and do not require special care. They die sometimes in the process of being stuck on the way out, but once they get here alive, they usually are healthy. SGA puppies sometimes require a bit of supplementation, some glucose and a more watchful eye, but they also do well. Often the SGA puppies latch on to a nipple like little kangaroos and just seem to stay in place day after day.

The main thing to remember about LGA and SGA puppies is this. The size you see on the day of whelping is influenced not by the size of the sire or the size of the dam, but by the quality of the implant site that the egg found within the uterine horns. The three little Cavalier puppies pictured here are great examples of the impact of uterine implant and how it effects puppy size on day of delivery. Obviously, the large girl (far right) implanted into an outstanding site within the uterus. Her placenta was able to tap into a maximum blood supply from mom and she received great nutrition from the day she implanted. She was, as you might have guessed, the first puppy born. She is a perfect example of how the puppies in the portion of the uterine horn located closest to the vulva become very large. The large tri-colored girl (middle) was born second and the tiny little tri-colored girl was the last puppy whelped. The same dog sired all three puppies. Sometimes large puppies continue on to become larger than normal dogs and other times they are normal sized adults. It is not unusual for the largest puppy at birth to become the smallest dog when the litter reaches adulthood. It is the same with the SGA puppies. Sometimes they stay very tiny (this one did) and other times they grow to normal size. There is no predicting what will happen. This remarkable difference in size at birth is not caused by genetics, rather it is created by the quality of the implant site within the uterus.

## How do we know that that we are not seeing genetics at work day of whelping?

There is an easy answer to this question. The answer is that Mother Nature realized that the canine would come in several different sizes and shapes and that sperm from any dog can fertilize eggs ovulated by any bitch. She knew that occasionally a very limber and determined German Shepherd boy could conceivably breed a very short sighted and long-backed Dachshund girl. The bitch was designed so that her own size will limit, to a great degree, how large her puppies can be. It undoubtedly is not true 100% of the time, but it is true the vast majority of the time. Dogs have more genetic diversity than any other mammal coming in all shapes, all colors and an amazing range of sizes from three-pound toys all the way up to 220-pound giants. Because of the wide range in size, and the certainty that any dog's sperm can be used to penetrate any bitch's egg, birth weights of puppies are governed by the size of the mom. This is not the case in mammals such as horses, cattle and pigs. Those animals, while still enjoying a degree of genetic diversity certainly do not have the tremendous variations in size that dogs do. Premies often attain full size; SGA puppies often stay quite small.

## I think I have run out of things to say…maybe

When it comes to our dogs and how they breed and how we can get their puppies to thrive, I will probably never run out of things to say and I will never run out of things to learn. As long as there are dog breeders out there who are willing to take the time to teach me things and share with me, I am willing to learn. As long as I am able to do so, I will continue to give seminars when I am invited and be available to all of you who need me for support. If I can help a single breeder have a successful breeding or save a puppy, then I am happy and content. I love hearing your success stories about whelping and saving your puppies. I never get tired of knowing what you did and how you did it. Please be supportive to one another. In our society, there is very little support for dog breeders. People simply do not want us breeding our dogs, not even most of our vets. If we do not give support to one another, there will be no place to turn. If you need me, I am easy to reach at my email address: myrasavant@hotmail.com and you can always re-stock your breeding, whelping and puppy care supplies at my web site: www.myrasavantharris.com.

# APPENDIX
# LAB TESTS

## What Do Lab Tests Tell the Vet?

During the years when I worked as a nurse, I frequently heard patients complaining about all the tests that their physicians had ordered. They particularly disliked blood tests and often considered them an unnecessary expense. Blood tests and other diagnostic tests, while admittedly sometimes expensive, give your vet more information than most of you realize. They are quite the little bargain when you take into consideration all of the things that your vet can learn about your dog and the health of his body and organs from a simple little blood draw. Both you and your vet truly hit the informational jackpot when blood is tested. For the sake of certainty, blood tests are the diagnostic bargains of the medical world. As the treatment plan for your dog is put into effect, do not be surprised if your vet orders repeat blood work because the results of those tests will be the best indication of whether the treatment is working or not. The vet can follow the progress of the treatment by looking at his blood values.

Before I discuss lab values and what they mean with you, it is important for me to remind you that each dog, and even certain breeds of dogs, will have differing test results and are still considered normal. Whether the number that comes back shows your dog to be at the high end of normal or the low end of normal, normal means exactly what it says—normal for your particular dog on the particular day the blood was drawn. The blood is usually drawn from a vein (veins carry blood back to the heart) versus an artery (arteries carry freshly oxygenated blood away from the heart). Although there are some important blood tests that must be drawn from an artery, such as those that show the blood gases, veins are more toward the surface of the body and arteries are deeper in the muscles and tissues. Veins do not have a pulse, but arteries do. Discomfort during the blood draw is minimal and the risks are almost nonexistent. Watch the site for a day or two for signs of infection, but this rarely happens.

In order for all of the components of the blood test to be accurate, you need to avoid feeding the dog for the twelve hours prior to the blood draw. If you are scheduling a vet's appointment, it is probably a good idea to schedule a morning appointment and plan to feed the dog after you have seen the vet. This way, if your vet does decide to draw blood the tests will be more accurate. You can save some time if you collect a small stool sample before you go to the vet's office and with very little effort, you can collect a urine sample as well. Forget that nonsense about following the dog around with a pie tin taped to a stick. There is an easy way to collect a urine sample.

Here is how you can collect urine and have a fresh sample for your vet in case it is needed. If it is not needed, it can be discarded:

1. Wash the penis or vulva with warm water and a little bit of soap. Rinse. This will get the area clean, but it will not be sterile. Do this before you walk the dog, first thing in the morning.

2. Dry the area with a hair dryer.

3. Using two-sided scotch tape, put tape around the top edges of a baggie (size dependent upon the size of your dog) and simply tape the bag to the genital area. The two-sided tape makes this easy. You may need to use a large amount of two-sided tape to attach it securely.

4. Walk the dog on a leash until the dog urinates in the bag. Remove the bag quickly, making sure all of the tape removed completely and transfer the urine to a container that can be safely closed.

## Blood tests

The tubes that contain the blood have different colored stoppers that give instant visual recognition of what those particular tubes contain and what the tests blood inside the tubes will undergo. They are color coded. Do not be surprised if your vet or vet tech draws enough blood to fill more than one or two tubes. The different tests require different chemicals for processing and often the chemicals are contained in the tubes themselves. The most common blood test is probably a CBC—Complete Blood Count. The CBC will give your vet a lot of information about your dog's blood. Each piece of information that is gathered will be put together somewhat like a puzzle to assist your vet in diagnosing what is happening in your dog's body.

# Analyzing blood test results

### Red Blood Cells (RBC)
Normal: 5.5 to 8.5—Red blood cells are the cells that are responsible for carrying oxygen molecules throughout the body to nourish and strengthen it. If the lab value shows that the RBC count is low, it will be a clue that perhaps your dog does not have enough iron in his blood. If the count is quite low, it may indicate that the dog has had a hemorrhage. Sometimes you can see the blood coming out of the body and other times it is all internal, so you can only tell that the dog is sick, but you can't actually see signs of bleeding. A low RBC can also be an indication of bone marrow disease, parasites or a deficiency of vitamin B-12. If the blood tests show low RBCs and there is no indication of hemorrhage, the problem may be a long-term problem. More

blood tests will help the vet to find out what that long-term problem might be. Red blood cells live for around 120 days and are constantly manufactured in the bone marrow.

### Hematocrit (HCT) or Packed Cell Volume (PVC)

Normal: 0.37 to 0.55—Decreased levels are a red flag for anemia, which can be caused by hemorrhage, parasites, poor diet or a chronic disease process such as cancer or liver disease. Increased levels are often a clear indication of dehydration. As the amount of fluid in the blood decreases with dehydration, the HCT will increase because now the blood cells are more concentrated in less fluid.

### Hemoglobin (HgB)

Normal: 120-180—Hemoglobin is the substance in the blood that carries molecules of oxygen. Decreased levels might indicate the presence of hemorrhage, anemia or iron deficiency. Increased levels would be a sign that there are higher than normal amounts of RBCs in the blood or B-12 deficiency.

### Reticulocytes

Normal: 0 to 1.5%—Reticulocytes are immature red blood cells. An increase in the count is associated with chronic hemorrhage (possible internal bleeding) or hemolytic anemia. A decreased count is usually associated with some type of leukemia.

### Platelets (PLT)

Normal: 2 to 9—Platelets play an important role in blood clotting. Increased numbers may occur with fracture of the bones, an injury to the vascular system or cancer. A decrease of platelets often occurs in autoimmune hemolytic anemia, lupus, hemorrhage or coagulation within the vascular system.

### MCV

Normal: 60 to 77—This is a measurement of the average size of the red blood cells (RBC). Decreased values are almost always a sign of iron deficiency. Increased values are frequently a sign of B-12 (folic acid) deficiency.

### White Blood Cells (WBC)

Normal: 6.0 to 17.1—White blood cells are the body's first defense against infection. If there are increased levels, your vet will look for a *bacterial* infection, extreme stress and some blood disorders. If the levels are decreased, it is a sign of *viral* infections or possibly drug or chemical poisoning. Decreased WBCs are a sign of viral infection because the viruses target WBCs, "inject" them with their own DNA and turn them into little manufacturing plants for the virus. Over time the number of WBCs becomes severely decreased as they have all been used for virus manufacturing. The body's response to bacteria is just to send as many WBC's as possible to the site so the numbers are increased in bacterial infections. Bacteria replicate themselves by dividing only. Antibiotics usually work by interfering with the process of bacterial replication although some work more directly by killing the bacteria. None of them kill viruses.

## Lymphocytes (L/M)

Normal: 1.0 to 4.8—This particular type of white blood cell is rounded and smooth. They increase with chronic infections, or as the dog recovers from an acute infection. They go down in numbers at times of extreme stress or if the dog has been treated with steroids or chemotherapy.

## Calcium (CA)

Normal: 9.5 to 12.0—Blood calcium levels are influenced by diet, but will not always be seen on a blood test because the increased calcium will be stored in the bone instead of circulating in the blood stream. Calcium levels are also affected by hormone levels, (particularly parathyroid hormone) and blood protein levels. Decreased calcium levels might point to disease of the pancreas as well. Muscle twitches might be seen and in severe cases the dog may suffer from ataxia, or the inability to control the muscles. Some types of tumors will also cause increased calcium levels as well as parathyroid or kidney disease.

## Progesterone

A level under five indicates that the bitch has not yet ovulated. A level of five or over indicates that ovulation has occurred. A level of under five in a gestated female is an indication that delivery may be at hand.

## Phosphorus

Normal: 3.3 to 6.8—Diet, parathyroid hormone and the kidneys affect phosphorus levels. Increased levels indicate an under active parathyroid gland and kidney failure. Decreased levels of phosphorus are an indication of an over active parathyroid gland and some types of cancer, malnutrition or the inability of the dog's body to absorb the chemical (malabsorption).

## Electrolytes (Sodium, Potassium and Chloride)

- Normal sodium: 140 to151

- Normal potassium: 3.4 to 5.4

- Normal chloride:105 to 120

Our bodies depend on the electrolyte supply for just about every cellular activity. Their importance can't be stressed enough. Their levels are particularly affected by vomiting or diarrhea because stomach acids are an important source of electrolytes. Electrolytes are also extremely important in cardiac function. It doesn't take many episodes of vomiting or diarrhea to cause a severe impact on the electrolyte balance in the body. *Decreased electrolyte levels can lead to death,* particularly in puppies.

## Cholesterol (CHOL)

Normal: 110 to 314—Increased levels of cholesterol are found in several disorders including hypothyroidism (under active thyroid gland), liver, kidney, or cardiovascular disease, diabetes and extreme stress. Decreased levels of cholesterol might indicate an overactive thyroid gland or intestinal malabsorption.

**Alanine Aminotransferase (ALT)**
Normal: 10 to 70—This is an enzyme that elevates with liver disease.

**Alkaline Phosphatase (ALKP)**
Normal: 20 to 200—ALKP is an enzyme that is produced in the liver. Levels will increase in the presence of liver disease or a block in the bile flow system.

**Total Billirubin (TBIL)**
Normal: .04 to .40—Bilirubin is one of the components of bile. It is secreted by the liver into the intestinal tract. Jaundice or yellowing of the whites of the eyes or skin is an indication of disease or destruction of the liver or the bile flow system.

**Total Protein (TP)**
Normal: 5.2 to 7.2—Elevated levels are a sign of dehydration or bone marrow or blood cancers. Decreases in these levels can indicate malnutrition, malabsorption, poor digestion, poor diet, bleeding or burns. (A lot of blood values go up in the presence of burns because as the cells are destroyed by the burns they release their contents into the blood stream.)

**Globulins (GLOBS)**
Normal: 0.9 to 4.0—Decreased levels raise red flags on the immune system and can be a sign of antibody problems, immune system problems, viral diseases or the risk of infectious disease. Increased levels can indicate dehydration, cancers, extreme stress, allergies, liver disorder, cardiovascular disease, arthritis or diabetes.

**Albumin (ALB)**
Normal: 2.5 to 4.3—Albumin levels can give your vet an idea of the nutritional status of your dog. Albumin is produced by the liver so decreased levels can indicate liver disease or kidney disease as well as parasitic infections such as hookworm. Higher levels point to dehydration and loss of protein.

**Blood Urea Nitrogen (BUN)**
Normal: 6 to 24—Blood urea nitrogen is produced by the liver and excreted by the kidneys. Lower levels are seen with low protein diets, liver failure and steroid use. Higher levels may indicate a condition that reduces the kidney's ability to filter body fluids or interferes with protein breakdown. (Dogs with kidney disease will often be put on a lower protein diet for this reason.)

**Creatinine (CREA)**
Normal: 0.4 to 1.4—Creatinine is a by-product of muscle metabolism and is excreted by the kidneys. Elevated levels can indicate kidney disease or an obstruction in the urinary system, muscle diseases, arthritis, hyperthyroidism (an over active thyroid gland) and diabetes. If the lab results show an increased BUN, but a normal Creatinine level it will suggest an early or mild problem. If the results show increased Creatinine, BUN and elevated phosphorus it will suggest a long standing kidney disease.

## Blood Glucose (GLU)

Normal: 65 to 120—Blood glucose is called "blood sugar." High levels can indicate diabetes, extreme stress, an excess level of progesterone or an over active adrenal gland. It is also elevated in burn cases. Low levels of blood glucose are an indication of liver disease, tumors or other abnormal growths on the pancreas or an under active adrenal gland.

## Amylase (AMYL)

Normal: 200 to 1290—The pancreas produces amylase to aid in digestion of foods. Elevated levels in the blood can indicate pancreatic and/or kidney disease.

# What your vet will look for in a urinalysis

Your vet may also order a urinalysis. For this test, you will need a urine sample from the dog. *This* can often be trickier than urine tests for humans because dogs don't usually cooperate and pee in a cup (preferring instead, their favorite little potty behind the couch). I've read directions on collecting urine on a dog by following the dog around with a pie tin duct taped on to a stick…but, for crying out loud, before you resort to a pie tin on a stick try the technique described in Chapter 10. This method can be used on little puppies too, but you will need to use one of those very small plastic bags with the zip lock top. These bags are sold in places like Office Depot and come in a variety of sizes. Once you have the collection, you can draw it up into a syringe for safe and clean transport to the vet.

If you are unable to collect the urine, your vet may decide to attempt to collect it by application of pressure to the bladder or with a catheter. It is also possible to collect urine by placing a needle directly into the bladder from outside the body.

## Color

The normal color is yellow to amber. If the color is too dark or orange, it is usually a clear sign of dehydration. Red or red streaks in the urine are caused by blood and are usually a sign of an infection of the bladder. Dark yellow to brown are caused by Bilirubin and reddish brown is caused by hemoglobin.

## Clarity

Normal urine is clear. Cloudiness is caused by crystals, cells, blood, bacteria, mucous or cast.

## Specific Gravity

Normal: 1.013-1.030—The specific gravity of the urine can be an indication of a number of things. If the specific gravity is very low, it may show that the dog has diabetes which is often first noticed as the dog's desire to drink lots of water. Low specific gravity may show that the kidneys are unable to concentrate urine. If the specific gravity is high, it may be a clear indicator of dehydration, particularly in puppies. The dehydration may be caused by vomiting, diarrhea, diabetes or high fever. One test is probably only an indicator or a red flag. Subsequent tests may prove to be normal and in that case, you can assume that the first abnormal test was simply a result of hydration status. In dogs, you can consider a specific gravity of 1.013 to 1.030 to be normal, although a level of 1.030 might be an indication of mild dehydration. 1.031 to 1.040 is a clear indication of dehydration and 1.007 to 1.012 can be a sign of kidney failure.

### PH Level
Normal: 6.2 to 6.5—PH measures the acidity of the urine.

### Ketones
Ketones should not be in the urine. If ketones are present, it is an indication of an imbalance of carbohydrates in the diet. Feed more carbs.

### Glucose
Glucose should not be in the urine. If glucose is present, it is an indication of diabetes.

Just remember that all of the ranges listed as normal are just that—normal. Dogs and their lab results vary from breed to breed and from individual to individual. Your particular dog may have lightly "abnormal" lab results that are actually totally normal for him.

# Supply Order Form

Prices include USPS postage to all US addresses. Email myrasavant@hotmail.com for questions.

Puppy Intensive Care/Canine Repro Book Set..... $55.00     quantity_____     Price_____

Puppy Rescue Kit.................................................$112.00     quantity_____     Price_____

Acetyl L Carnitine...............................................$18.00     quantity_____     Price_____

A.I. Kits (Small, Medium, Large)........................ $26.00     sz/quantity_____     Price_____

DeLee Mucus Traps2........................................... $18.00     quantity_____     Price_____

Fenegreek.............................................................$21.00     quantity_____     Price_____

Fertile Focus........................................................$56.00     quantity_____     Price_____

Glycoflex.............................................................$51.00     quantity_____     Price_____

Oral Calcium Plus............................................... $31.00     quantity_____     Price_____

Pink Stuff............................................................$21.00     quantity_____     Price_____

Stuck Puppy Kit...................................................$31.00     quantity_____     Price_____

## ALL ITEMS ORDERED MUST INCLUDE THE FOLLOWING:

NAME_____

ADDRESS (*Must be same as billing address)_____

City, State and ZIP _____

Phone #_____Email_____

(If paying by credit card you must include the following information)

Credit Card Type_____Number_____

Exp Date_____CVC_____Exact name on card_____

Mail to:
    Myra Harris
    1561 Weathervane Ct
    Fircrest, WA 98466

For Office Use Only:
CC data entered_____
Verify_____

**From Dogwise Publishing**
www.dogwise.com
1-800-776-2665

*BEHAVIOR & TRAINING*

**ABC's of Behavior Shaping. Proactive Behavior Mgmt,** DVD set. Ted Turner

**Aggression In Dogs. Practical Mgmt, Prevention, & Behaviour Modification.** Brenda Aloff

**Am I Safe? DVD.** Sarah Kalnajs

**Barking. The Sound of a Language.** Turid Rugaas

**Behavior Problems in Dogs, 3rd ed.** William Campbell

**Brenda Aloff's Fundamentals: Foundation Training for Every Dog, DVD.** Brenda Aloff

**Bringing Light to Shadow. A Dog Trainer's Diary.** Pam Dennison

**Canine Body Language. A Photographic Guide to the Native Language of Dogs.** Brenda Aloff

**Changing People Changing Dogs. Positive Solutions for Difficult Dogs. Rev.** Dee Ganley

**Chill Out Fido! How to Calm Your Dog.** Nan Arthur

**Clicked Retriever.** Lana Mitchell

**Do Over Dogs. Give Your Dog a Second Chance for a First Class Life.** Pat Miller

**Dog Behavior Problems. The Counselor's Handbook.** William Campbell

**Dog Friendly Gardens, Garden Friendly Dogs.** Cheryl Smith

**Dog Language, An Encyclopedia of Canine Behavior.** Roger Abrantes

**Dogs are from Neptune.** Jean Donaldson

**Evolution of Canine Social Behavior, 2nd ed.** Roger Abrantes

**From Hoofbeats to Dogsteps. A Life of Listening to and Learning from Animals.** Rachel Page Elliott

**Get Connected With Your Dog,** book with DVD. Brenda Aloff

**Give Them a Scalpel and They Will Dissect a Kiss, DVD.** Ian Dunbar

**Guide to Professional Dog Walking And Home Boarding.** Dianne Eibner

**How to Run a Dog Business. Putting Your Career Where Your Heart Is.** Veronica Boutelle

**Language of Dogs, DVD.** Sarah Kalnajs

**Mastering Variable Surface Tracking, Component Tracking (2 bk set).** Ed Presnall

**Minding Your Dog Business. A Practical Guide to Business Success for Dog Professionals.** Veronica Boutelle and Rikke Jorgensen

**My Dog Pulls. What Do I Do?** Turid Rugaas

**New Knowledge of Dog Behavior (reprint).** Clarence Pfaffenberger

**Oh Behave! Dogs from Pavlov to Premack to Pinker.** Jean Donaldson

**On Talking Terms with Dogs. Calming Signals, 2nd edition.** Turid Rugaas

**On Talking Terms with Dogs. What Your Dog Tells You, DVD.** Turid Rugaas

**Play With Your Dog.** Pat Miller

**Positive Perspectives. Love Your Dog, Train Your Dog.** Pat Miller

**Positive Perspectives 2. Know Your Dog, Train Your Dog.** Pat Miller

**Predation and Family Dogs, DVD.** Jean Donaldson

**Really Reliable Recall. Train Your Dog to Come When Called, DVD.** Leslie Nelson

**Right on Target. Taking Dog Training to a New Level.** Mandy Book & Cheryl Smith

**Stress in Dogs.** Martina Scholz & Clarissa von Reinhardt

**Tales of Two Species. Essays on Loving and Living With Dogs.** Patricia McConnell

**The Dog Trainer's Resource. The APDT Chronicle of the Dog Collection.** Mychelle Blake (*ed*)

**The Dog Trainer's Resource 2. The APDT Chronicle of the Dog Collection.** Mychelle Blake (*ed*)

**The Thinking Dog. Crossover to Clicker Training.** Gail Fisher

**Therapy Dogs. Training Your Dog To Reach Others.** Kathy Diamond Davis

**Training Dogs. A Manual (reprint).** Konrad Most

**Training the Disaster Search Dog.** Shirley Hammond

**Try Tracking. The Puppy Tracking Primer.** Carolyn Krause

**Visiting the Dog Park, Having Fun, and Staying Safe.** Cheryl S. Smith

**When Pigs Fly. Train Your Impossible Dog.** Jane Killion

**Winning Team. A Guidebook for Junior Showmanship.** Gail Haynes

**Working Dogs (reprint).** Elliot Humphrey & Lucien Warner

*HEALTH & ANATOMY, SHOWING*

**An Eye for a Dog. Illustrated Guide to Judging Purebred Dogs.** Robert Cole

**Annie On Dogs!** Ann Rogers Clark

**Another Piece of the Puzzle.** Pat Hastings

**Canine Cineradiography DVD.** Rachel Page Elliott

**Canine Massage. A Complete Reference Manual.** Jean-Pierre Hourdebaigt

**Canine Terminology (reprint).** Harold Spira

**Breeders Professional Secrets. Ethical Breeding Practices.** Sylvia Smart

**Dog In Action (reprint).** Macdowell Lyon

**Dog Show Judging. The Good, the Bad, and the Ugly.** Chris Walkowicz

**Dogsteps DVD.** Rachel Page Elliott

**The Healthy Way to Stretch Your Dog. A Physical Theraphy Approach.** Sasha Foster and Ashley Foster

**The History and Management of the Mastiff.** Elizabeth Baxter & Pat Hoffman

**Performance Dog Nutrition. Optimize Performance With Nutrition.** Jocelynn Jacobs

**Positive Training for Show Dogs. Building a Relationship for Success** Vicki Ronchette

**Puppy Intensive Care. A Breeder's Guide To Care Of Newborn Puppies.** Myra Savant Harris

**Raw Dog Food. Make It Easy for You and Your Dog.** Carina MacDonald

**Raw Meaty Bones.** Tom Lonsdale

**Shock to the System. The Facts About Animal Vaccination...** Catherine O'Driscoll

**Tricks of the Trade. From Best of Intentions to Best in Show, Rev. Ed.** Pat Hastings

**Work Wonders. Feed Your Dog Raw Meaty Bones.** Tom Lonsdale

**Whelping Healthy Puppies, DVD.** Sylvia Smart

Dogwise.com is your complete
source for dog books on the web!

2,000+ titles, fast shipping, and
excellent customer service.

Dogwise now has over 100 eBooks
and we are adding more every week!

**Dogwise** All things dog.

| Welcome | Featured Titles | Shows & Info | Publishing | Bargain Books | Help/Contact |

Phone in your Order! 1.800.776.2665 8am-4pm PST / 11am-7pm EST

**Be the First to Hear the News!**
Have New Product and Promotion
Announcements Emailed to You.
Click Here To Sign Up!

Free Shipping for Orders over $75 - click here for more information!

Win a $25 Dogwise credit - click here to find out how!

**Featured New Titles**

**STRESS IN DOGS - LEARN HOW DOGS SHOW STRESS AND WHAT YOU CAN DO TO HELP,** by Martina Scholz & Clarissa von Reinhardt
Item: DTB909
Is stress causing your dog's behavior problems? Research shows that as with humans, many behavioral problems in dogs are stress-related. Learn how to recognize when your dog is stressed, what factors cause stress in dogs, and strategies you can utilize in training and in your daily life with your dog to reduce stress.
Price: $14.95 more information...
DIG IN

**SUCCESS IS IN THE PROOFING - A GUIDE FOR CREATIVE AND EFFECTIVE TRAINING,** by Debby Quigley & Judy Ramsey
Item: DTO230
The success is indeed in the proofing! Proofing is an essential part of training, but one that is often overlooked or not worked on enough. We all know the story of the dog who can perform a variety of behaviors perfectly in the backyard but falls apart in the obedience ring. This book is full of great ideas and strategies to help your dog do his best no matter what the distractions or conditions may be. Whether competing in Rally or Obedience, trainers everywhere will find this very portable and user friendly book an indispensable addition to their tool box.
Price: $19.95 more information...
DIG IN

**REALLY RELIABLE RECALL DVD,** by Leslie Nelson
Item: DTB810P
From well-known trainer Leslie Nelson! Easy to follow steps to train your dog to come when it really counts, in an emergency. Extra chapters for difficult to train breeds and training class instructors.
Price: $29.95 more information...
DIG IN

**THE DOG TRAINERS RESOURCE - APDT CHRONICLE OF THE DOG COLLECTION,** by Mychelle Blake, Editor
Item: DTB880
The modern professional dog trainer needs to develop expertise in a wide variety of fields: learning theory, training techniques, classroom strategies, marketing, community relations, and business development and management. This collection of articles from APDT's Chronicle of the Dog will prove a valuable resource for trainers and would-be trainers.
Price: $24.95 more information...
 DIG IN

**SHAPING SUCCESS - THE EDUCATION OF AN UNLIKELY CHAMPION,** by Susan Garrett
Item: DTA260
Written by one of the world's best dog trainers, Shaping Success gives an excellent explanation of the theory behind animal learning as Susan Garrett trains a high-energy Border Collie puppy to be an agility champion. Buzzy's story both entertains and demonstrates how to apply some of the most up-to-date dog training methods in the real world. Clicker training!
Price: $24.95 more information...
 DIG IN

**FOR THE LOVE OF A DOG - UNDERSTANDING EMOTION IN YOU AND YOUR BEST FRIEND,** by Patricia McConnell
Item: DTB890
Sure to be another bestseller, Trish McConnell's latest book takes a look at canine emotions and body language. Like all her books, this one is written in a way that the average dog owner can follow but brings the latest scientific information that trainers and dog enthusiasts can use.
Price: $24.95 more information...
 DIG IN

**HELP FOR YOUR FEARFUL DOG: A STEP-BY-STEP GUIDE TO HELPING YOUR DOG CONQUER HIS FEARS,** by Nicole Wilde
Item: DTB878
From popular author and trainer Nicole Wilde! A comprehensive guide to the treatment of canine anxiety, fears, and phobias. Chock full of photographs and illustrations and written in a down-to-earth, humorous style.
Price: $24.95 more information...
 DIG IN

**FAMILY FRIENDLY DOG TRAINING - A SIX WEEK PROGRAM FOR YOU AND YOUR DOG,** by Patricia McConnell & Aimee Moore
Item: DTB917
A six-week program to get people and dogs off on the right paw! Includes trouble-shooting tips for what to do when your dog doesn't respond as expected. This is a book that many trainers will want their students to read.
Price: $11.95 more information...
 DIG IN

**THE LANGUAGE OF DOGS - UNDERSTANDING CANINE BODY LANGUAGE AND OTHER COMMUNICATION SIGNALS DVD SET,** by Sarah Kalnajs
Item: DTB875P
Features a presentation and extensive footage of a variety of breeds showing hundreds of examples of canine behavior and body language. Perfect for dog owners or anyone who handles dogs or encounters them regularly while on the job.
Price: $39.95 more information...
 DIG IN